CULTURES OF THE WORLD

SINGAPORE

Lesley Layton

MARSHALL CAVENDISH
New York • London • Sydney

Reference edition published 1990 by
Marshall Cavendish Corporation
2415 Jerusalem Avenue
P.O. Box 587
North Bellmore
New York 11710

© Times Editions Pte Ltd 1994, 1990

Originated and designed by
Times Books International, an imprint of
Times Editions Pte Ltd

Printed in Singapore

Library of Congress Cataloging-in-Publication Data:
Layton, Lesley, 1954–
    Singapore / Lesley Layton.
        p. cm.—(Cultures Of The World)
    Includes bibliographical references.
    Summary: Introduces the geography, history,
    religious beliefs, government, and people of
    Singapore.
    ISBN 1-85435-295-4
    1. Singapore—Juvenile literature.
[1. Singapore.] I. Title. II. Series.
DS598.S7L35 1990
959.57—dc20   89–25465
                CIP
                    AC

Cultures of the World

Editorial Director	Shirley Hew
Managing Editor	Shova Loh
Editors	Falaq Kagda
	Winnifred Wong
	Tan Kok Eng
	Azra Moiz
	Len Webster
	Mario Sismondo
	Elizabeth Koh-Kanematsu
	Jo-Ann Kee
	Saw Myat Yin
	Sue Sismondo
Picture Editor	Mee-Yee Lee
Production	Edmund Lam
Design	Tuck Loong
	Ronn Yeo
	Felicia Wong
	Loo Chuan Ming
Illustrators	Francis Oak
	Thomas Koh
	Vincent Chew
	William Sim
	Lok Kerk Hwang
	Tan Suat Lin
MCC Editorial Director	Evelyn M. Fazio
MCC Production Manager	Ruth Toda

INTRODUCTION

SINGAPORE, a tiny island 1° north of the Equator, lies at the tip of the Asian mainland, just south of Thailand and Malaysia. This strategic position, together with a natural harbor, has enabled the 19th century fishing village to flourish into the modern city it is today.

Modern Singapore was founded in 1819 when the British started a trading post on the island. Migrants from China, India, the Middle East, and Europe came to the bustling port. Their descendants made the island one of the busiest ports in the world, a financial center for the region, and a tourist destination. It's expanding economy and industries have transformed the country few thought would survive into one of the four "Asian Tigers."

Yet despite all its modernity, much of traditional Singapore still remains. Singaporeans still celebrate the festivals of their ancestors, marry according to age-old customs, and enjoy the foods of the original migrants. This book is part of a series, *Cultures of the World*, that takes a look at people and their lifestyles around the world.

CONTENTS

Chinese worshipers burning joss sticks in prayer

CONTENTS

Top: **The king of fruits, the durian**

Bottom: **Winning entries in a children's art competition**

GEOGRAPHY

THE REPUBLIC OF SINGAPORE lies at the southern tip of Peninsular Malaysia. Besides the main island of Singapore, there are also 58 offshore islets. Settlements of wood and zinc huts on stilts are still to be found on some of these islets, but the residents are gradually being relocated to the main island. Other islets play an important economic role, either as locations for oil refineries or pleasure resorts.

TOPOGRAPHY

The main island of Singapore is made up of three different regions: high land in the center, a gently undulating area in the west, and a flat eastern region. Between the coasts and the remaining forests lies open country, with the city to the south and the parks, gardens, and agricultural land mainly to the north.

"It is impossible to conceive a place combining more advantages; it is within a week's sail of China, still closer to Siam, Cochin-China, in the very heart of the Archipelago, or as the Malays call it, 'the Navel of the Malay countries.'"

—Sir Stamford Raffles, founder of modern Singapore

THE REPUBLIC OF SINGAPORE

Singapore is 85 miles north of the equator and is the Asian city nearest to it. The island's coastline of about 85 miles encloses a land area of 224 square miles. Including the offshore islets, Singapore's total area is 247 square miles and growing: land is constantly being reclaimed from the sea, and seven southern islets are to be merged by the year 2010. The highest point is the Bukit Timah Nature Reserve, which is 544 feet above sea level.

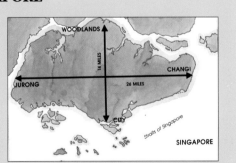

Opposite: **Singapore's skyscrapers dominate its coastline. Its position at the southern extremity of the Malay Peninsula has enabled it to become a thriving modern city-state, with the second-highest standard of living in Asia.**

RIVERS

Despite its unimpressive size, the Singapore River has always been the center of any settlement on the island because of its vital role in trade, the country's lifeblood. The river flows into a wide natural harbor where its calm waters still allow undisturbed anchorage for small vessels.

In the past, trading boats crammed the harbor, but when large steamships were introduced, tidal changes made it unsuitable. The ships moved to the deep narrow waterway between the main island and Sentosa, the largest of the offshore islands. Meanwhile, small barges or "bumboats" continued to ply the river to bring goods inland.

Once the center of noisy activity, the river has now been cleaned and cleared of traffic. Some warehouses that once stored cargo survive along its edges but have been converted for other uses. The quay is being livened up by landscaping, and pleasure cruises upriver have been introduced.

Other rivers, such as the Kallang and its tributaries, act as catchment areas over which dams have been built to create artificial lakes that store rainwater. The oldest and largest reservoirs are located on high ground in the center of the island to catch the heaviest rainfall, while newer reservoirs along the west coast provide water to homes and factories sprouting up in that part of the island.

There are now 14 reservoirs and not enough land to accommodate more, so water is carefully conserved. Much of it must be bought from the state of Johor in the south of Malaysia to meet the demands of Singapore's expanding population. Unlike many other Asian countries, Singapore's water is chemically treated, so it is safe to drink it straight from the tap.

Aerial view of MacRitchie Reservoir from where water was first piped into the city in 1857. This reservoir is an important source of water supply for the island. Close to the city, it also offers a green refuge in a built-up environment as its grounds are maintained as a nature reserve.

THE CITY

Over the years the focal point of the city has shifted back from the shoreline and has been replaced by the Central Business District, an area of high-rise offices, banks, stores, and restaurants. The city center now lies behind this, among hotels and department stores. Scattered around the city are the industrial areas and a series of small satellite towns, each with its own services and facilities.

Singapore prides itself on the "greening" program that has earned it the nickname of "Garden City." Trees and grassy areas have kept pace with the rapid growth of the city to soften the monotony of concrete. Statistics show there is now one tree for every fourth person on the island.

A network of roads and expressways crisscross the country. To lessen traffic problems in the inner city areas, the Mass Rapid Transit (MRT) system was introduced. Construction began in 1983, and by 1990 the MRT system was fully operational. Tracks and stations have been built above and below ground to connect the main housing areas with the city, allowing people to travel more comfortably and in a shorter time.

CLIMATE

The average daily temperature is 80°F, varying little more than a few degrees over the year. Unlike countries in the temperate zone, Singapore has no distinct seasons. Singapore lies in the path of two monsoons, causing rainfall all year round, but primarily during the northeast monsoon from November to January. In July, during the southwest monsoon, much of the rain falls in short showers interspersed with sunshine. In the months between monsoons, thunderstorms are common.

This hot, humid climate is due to the island's proximity to the equator and to its exposure to a sea lacking cold currents.

Above left: **The Mass Rapid Transit (MRT) system links the various satellite towns to the city center.**

Above right: **From the months of October/November to January, Singaporeans have to put up with very heavy rainstorms.**

An aerial view from the Bukit Timah Nature Reserve. Much of the island's original flora can be found in this protected area managed by the Nature Reserve Board.

FLORA AND FAUNA

Singapore's warm moist conditions also give rise to a lush natural vegetation that once covered the entire island. Much of this growth was cleared long ago for marine fish farming and timber products, leaving little swamp and meager patches of primary, secondary, and mangrove growth still on the island.

Modernization and land reclamation have been responsible for the loss of many wildlife species, but for its size Singapore still has one of the most varied ecological habitats in the world. A few stretches of seashore undisturbed by reclamation or development support reef coral, crabs, and various kinds of seaweed. The Singaporean freshwater species of crab is found nowhere else in the world.

Native plants are dwindling fast; most of Singapore's plants are imported species introduced mainly for shade and color. In its early years, the Singapore Botanic Gardens played an important role in fostering agricultural development in the region through collecting, growing, and distributing important plants, including—in 1877—the rubber plant from Ceylon.

The Bukit Timah Nature Reserve has the most concentrated number of indigenous plants, as well as small mammals, including the civet cat, the flying lemur, and the tree shrew. Creatures such as the leaf monkey, the mousedeer, and the wild boar died out long ago with the loss of their natural habitat. The tiger disappeared in the 1930s, the last one having been shot in 1932.

An expanse of swampland has been turned into a large bird sanctuary as Singapore is a haven for migrant birds from September to April each year. Someof the birds, like the Chinese egret, belong to internationally endangered species.

Reptiles ranging from the house gecko to the water monitor are common. There are 40 types of snakes, but only a few, such as the cobra and coral snake, are poisonous.

THE HOUSE GECKO

The island's best-known member of the lizard family is the harmless house gecko. Its feet are equipped with tiny hairs and claws, allowing it to run upside down along ceilings. It is one of the few wild creatures that can live harmoniously with people. Houses shelter it from outside predators, and in return the lizard consumes most of the insects attracted indoors by electric lights.

House geckos easily lose their tails. This is a ploy because the twitching of a shed tail usually startles an enemy long enough for the lizard to make its escape. A new tail always grows, but a series of bumps and ridges gives away the number of tails lost. The Malay name for the gecko is *cicak* ("chee-chak"), after the sound it makes. This loud clicking is familiar in Singapore homes, as are the gecko's fragile white eggs nestling behind bookcases and picture frames.

HISTORY

LITTLE IS KNOWN about ancient Singapore. One of the earliest references to Singapore comes from a Javanese account, the *Nagarakretagama*, that referred to a settlement called Temasek ("Sea Town") on the island. Chinese trade ships traveling between the South China Sea and the Straits of Malacca in Malaysia would break their journey at this conveniently located place. Early travelers' accounts describe it as a wild place, where piracy was a way of life.

By the 13th century, Temasek had a new name, Singapura, or "Lion City." A century later, Singapore was caught up in the prolonged conflict between Siam (Thailand) and the Java-based Majapahit Empire for control of the Malay Peninsula. A victim of the conflict, Singapore fell into decay and was to lie dormant until its reawakening in the early 19th century.

HOW THE ISLAND GOT ITS NAME

According to tradition, an Indian king, Raja Chulan, married a mermaid and had three sons, who later became rulers of kingdoms in Sumatra. The youngest, Sang Nila Utama, searched the nearby islands as possible sites for a new city and was particularly attracted by one. It was called Temasek.

As Sang Nila Utama and his men sailed toward the island, their ship was caught in a fierce storm and began to sink. To lighten their load, Sang Nila Utama threw his crown into the sea. Suddenly, the sea became calm and the men reached Temasek's shores in safety.

While exploring the island, they saw a strange animal. Sang Nila Utama was told that it was a lion.

Seeing such a strong, bold creature was a good omen. The king believed he had found the place to build a great city and decided to call it *Singapura*, "Lion City."

Opposite: **Sir Thomas Stamford Raffles was an employee of the British East India Company when he founded modern Singapore in 1819. In the short time he spent there, he began many projects that survive today. He believed edu-cation was important and began a school that later became the well-known Raffles Institution; his interest in plants and animals led to the first Botanic Gardens, and he started the Raffles Library and Museum in the building that is now the National Museum. He returned to England in 1823, a sick man. He died soon afterwards at the age of 45. His name lives on in many places in Singapore, one of which is the famous Raffles Hotel.**

EARLY HISTORY

Singapore became prominent about 1390, when Parameswara, a prince of Palembang in Sumatra, set himself up as ruler of the island after murdering his host, the chieftain. However, soon after, he was driven out in the struggle between neighboring countries for control of the Malay Peninsula and fled to Malacca (better known as Melaka today), where he founded the powerful Malaccan Sultanate.

A village settlement of the Orang Laut, off Pulau Brani. The dwellings of these boat people are built on stilts.

In the early 16th century, Malacca was captured by the Portuguese and the sultan escaped farther south to set up a new kingdom, the Johor-Riau Sultanate, that included Singapore. An outpost was established on the island only to be burned down by the Portuguese.

Until the early 19th century the island was deserted by traders and seamen and left once again to pirates and visiting boat people called Orang Laut. A few Malays and Chinese from the Riau Islands and some Orang Laut formed a village settlement (called a *kampung* in Malay) by the Singapore River, led by a temenggong, a senior minister of the Johor-Riau Sultanate.

On January 2, 1819, a British fleet led by Sir Thomas Stamford Raffles arrived on the island. They wanted to set up a trading post. The temenggong and the young sultan of Johor could not give their consent: by then the Dutch had control of Malacca and the Johor-Riau Sultanate. However, an elder brother was proclaimed the rightful sultan by the British and permission was granted through him instead. A ceremony followed to raise the British flag and mark the founding of modern Singapore.

POPULATION

When Raffles first arrived in 1819, Singapore was a small settlement of about 150 people. In 1824, Malays made up nearly three-quarters of the population. However, by 1867, the Chinese had firmly established themselves as the majority. In the 19th century there were almost no women on the island, but today the population shows a fairly even division between the sexes, with almost as many females (49.5%) as males (50.5%). The total population is almost 2.9 million, made up of 77.6% Chinese; 14.2% Malay; and 7.1% Indian; with a small group of mixed ethnicity. Since 1980, population figures have only been calculated on the basis of Singapore citizens and permanent residents. With a large number of foreign workers, domestic servants, and visitors, the population of the island at any time is likely to be over 3 million.

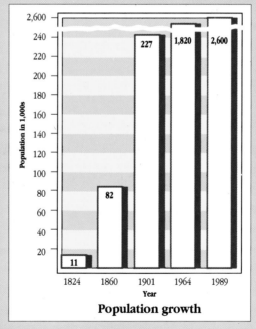

Population growth

POLITICAL HISTORY

Raffles thought Singapore the perfect answer to the British need for a port in the south of the Malay Peninsula. It would protect merchant ships in the area and prevent the Dutch from gaining further power over the lucrative East Indian spice trade.

In 1826, the British added Singapore to two other ports on the Malay Peninsula, Malacca and Penang, forming the Straits Settlements. All three were governed by British India until 1832, when Singapore became their center of government. In 1867, they were ruled from London as a single Crown Colony.

In 1914, all the Malay states including the Straits Settlements, came under British rule as British Malaya. This led to peace, an improvement in government, and trade between Malaya and Singapore. In 1923, a linking causeway and railway were built to extend these commercial ties.

The arrival of the steamship and the opening of the Suez Canal in 1869 made Singapore once again an important stopover for ships traveling between Europe and East Asia. At this time the island enjoyed unprecedented prosperity.

THE JAPANESE OCCUPATION During World War II, the Japanese wanted control over Southeast Asia's reserves of oil, rubber, tin, and other supplies. In February 1942, this prompted the Japanese capture of Singapore, a brutal occupation lasting three-and-a-half years. During this time, there was little foreign trade, resulting in poor business, high unemployment, and a shortage of food and medicine. It was a period of great hardship that resulted in a longing to be free from foreign rule.

When the Japanese surrendered in 1945, the British returned to Singapore. In the meantime, anti-Japanese groups had turned anti-British.

"Our object is not territory but trade, a commercial emporium ..."

—*Sir Stamford Raffles*

A tableau in the Sentosa Wax Museum depicts the Japanese surrender to the British forces in Singapore after the bombing of Hiroshima and Nagasaki.

Communists gained the support of students and workers and used them to provoke strikes and riots. In 1948, a state of emergency against communism was called that lasted until 1960.

A British governor and his advisers ruled the Straits Settlements separately from Malaya. This met with fierce opposition from local leaders due to Singapore's close commercial ties with the mainland. In 1955, new political parties and partial self-government marked the first move toward democracy. By 1959, Singapore had a government led by its own prime minister and his Cabinet, although it remained under British control.

In September 1963, Singapore merged with a group of Malayan territories to form the Federation of Malaysia, to expand the country's economy and to be free of British rule. However, Singapore and Malaysia could not agree, and Singapore became an independent country on August 9, 1965.

SOCIAL HISTORY

After the British set up a trading post in 1819, Singapore's new prosperity brought a huge influx of people from all over the region in search of work, trade, or an escape from warring conditions in their homelands. Immigration brought badly needed cheap labor, marking the beginning of Singapore's multiracial society.

The population increased rapidly, leading to new settlements in other parts of the island. The town became increasingly crowded, dirty, and disorganized, hindering its proper growth as an important city. Raffles drew up a town plan dividing it into a series of districts. He set aside a government area on the south bank and a commercial area for merchants and traders in the north, and resettled the main ethnic groups in separate residential areas along the coast.

In spite of these improvements, slum conditions prevailed and tropical diseases were rampant. The death rate was high, although by the early 20th century some public health services were provided and philanthropists had built hospitals for the poor. The Japanese Occupation and the steady rise in population caused living conditions to worsen, until town planning was reintroduced in the late 1940s under the Singapore Improvement Trust. By the 1960s, the Housing and Development Board (HDB) was set up to provide public housing on a large scale and to make the surrounding environment more attractive.

SECRET SOCIETIES

When Chinese immigrants first arrived in Singapore, they often joined secret societies to combat poverty and loneliness. In return for work and lodging, they had to obey specific rules and often became involved in gang fights or in the collection of "protection" money. Members who broke the rules were severely punished.

The Chinese Protectorate was set up in 1877 under William Pickering, a much respected man who both spoke and wrote various Chinese dialects. He was able to help the government deal with these secret societies until a law was passed to suppress the largest of them.

Other Chinese immigrants joined together in clans—friendly societies of people who came from the same district in China and shared a common dialect. Clan associations served the social needs of their members, most of whom had no families. These groups kept the immigrants in touch with people like themselves who helped one another in times of trouble. Many of these clans survive to this day. They have now evolved to meet the changing needs of their members, providing scholarships and classes to teach Chinese culture and customs, which help to make the younger generation aware of its heritage.

Opposite: **Singapore Town, as it was divided by Sir Stamford Raffles. The different ethnic migrant groups were placed in separate districts.**

Left: **Chinese clan associations, which were based on kinship and geographical ties, not only helped newly arrived immigrants to settle but also looked after the welfare of their members.**

GOVERNMENT

SINGAPORE'S LONG RULE by the British East India Company in the 19th century laid the foundations for its future government. Raffles set up the first laws, and they have until this day remained based on the British system, although they have been modified to meet the special requirements of a multiracial people. Government philosophy is also influenced by the Chinese system of ethics known as Confucianism.

NATIONAL GOVERNMENT

Singapore has a parliamentary system based on the British House of Commons, with a Parliamentary Act that states its powers and restrictions. Until 1993, a president was elected by Parliament every four years, but that year the Constitution was changed and Singaporeans themselves voted their fifth president, Ong Teng Cheong, into office.

Above: **An alumnus of Raffles Institution in Singapore and a law graduate of the University of Cambridge in England, Lee Kuan Yew was Singapore's leader from 1959 to 1990. He now holds the title of senior minister.**

Opposite: **Parliament House, the oldest government building in Singapore, is located in the city's civic district.**

The president is head of state and appoints a member of Parliament as prime minister and a group of ministers to form the Cabinet. Each minister is responsible for a different ministry, such as the Ministry of Defense, Law, and Education. The prime minister is the head of government, but under the recent constitutional changes, the elected president has important powers of veto over some decisions made by Parliament. The president, in consultation with the Presidential Council of Advisers, is responsible for appointing key civil servants.

The People's Action Party (PAP), formed on multiracial principles, was founded in 1954 and has remained in power since its historic election in 1959. Its leader, Lee Kuan Yew, probably exercised more influence over the people and saw more of his dreams for the country become a reality than any other head of government in the world.

Goh Chok Tong, an experienced minister from previous PAP governments, became prime minister of Singapore in November 1990 following the resignation of Lee Kuan Yew, who nevertheless continues to play an important part in public life.

Opposition to the PAP government exists, but there has been a lack of unity among those who oppose it. The government has often been criticized for its strict control over the print and broadcast media, including the circulation of magazines. As the government insists on a right of reply to published criticism, there has also been a series of conflicts with leading international newspapers and magazines.

Once Singapore became an independent nation in 1965, its citizens had to think of themselves as Singaporeans rather than British subjects or Malaysians. A sensitivity to issues of ideology, race, and language that divided society became crucial to the success of the new nation. Even with stability and prosperity, Singapore continues to search for a national ideology, a set of traditional values common to each community yet relevant to a modern society.

LOCAL AUTHORITIES

Singapore has many planned public housing estates built by a government agency, the Housing and Development Board. In each town, there are apartment blocks, schools, shopping facilities that range from markets to modern department stores, community centers, and factories. All these facilities make the new towns self-supporting. The Town Councils and Residents' Committees manage and maintain the public housing estates. They act as a channel through which decisions for the constituency can be made at a local level. Conversely, a government liaison officer maintains links with the Residents' Committees to make sure the public is kept in touch with national policies.

LEGAL STRUCTURES

Administration of justice is in the hands of the Supreme Court and the Subordinate Courts, which are basically independent of the government. However, an attorney-general and his legal officers advise the government on legal matters and perform legal duties assigned to them by the Cabinet.

The Supreme Court consists of the chief justice and judges appointed by the president on the advice of the prime minister. The Subordinate Court consists of district judges, magistrates, coroners, and small claims referees who are appointed by the president on the recommendation of the chief justice.

The death sentence is enforced in Singapore for trafficking in narcotics. Strict rules and rigorous government campaigns are regularly imposed on the public and some may appear unnecessarily restrictive to individual freedom. However, many Singaporeans regard these regulations simply as national needs drawn up by the government.

The Supreme Court Building is an example of colonial architecture in Singapore. Much ot the proceedings that are held within the building are also based on British laws.

ECONOMY

AS SINGAPORE HAS NO NATURAL RESOURCES worth exploiting other than its harbor and strategic location, its main resource is its people. When the first immigrants settled on the island of Singapore, they tended to fall into specific occupational groups. The bulk of the Chinese were traders and businessmen, the Malays fishermen and farmers, and the Indians merchants and moneylenders.

Over the years the population grew rapidly. New jobs had to be developed to employ a great many people, especially when it became clear that Singapore needed to produce goods that would be in demand in developed countries.

Today, the largest group of workers are employed in the manufacturing and commercial sectors. About 28% of the work force is found in factories as production operators, mechanics, and packers; less than 0.5% remain as farmers or fishermen.

Large businesses such as banking, insurance, and factory investment have created a rise in financial and business services. Singapore's location, efficient trading links, and political stability have attracted large foreign companies with a network of international markets. With their support, Singapore is becoming an international financial center.

Small businesses are also encouraged to contribute more effectively to the economy since they employ a large portion of the work force. To this end, several schemes, such as the Small Industry Technical Assistance Scheme and the Business Development Scheme, were set up.

Opposite: **An aerial view of an industrial town. When Singapore became independent, large-scale manufacturing industries such as these had to be started to provide jobs for the people. These were soon to become the source of the country's success.**

Below: **Many of the trades that began in the 19th century still exist today in places like Chinatown. This particular store deals with the importation of foodstuffs.**

27

INDUSTRIES

When Singapore became independent in 1965, it became clear that it needed to produce goods that would be in demand in developed countries. Large-scale manufacturing industries were started, which became the source of Singapore's success. A large percentage of workers had to be trained to handle the specialized equipment used. Today, there is no shortage of skilled workers, the result of investment in technical education.

The island is becoming increasingly attractive to Japanese and U.S. corporations that plan to install their operational headquarters overseas. The importance of this lies not just in the employment generated, but in the technology and skills that can be learned, though not at the expense of local expertise.

The republic is the most important oil-refining center in Southeast Asia, and one of the largest in the world. Crude oil is brought to Singapore from Malaysia, Brunei, Indonesia, and the Middle East, refined into many grades for different purposes, and re-exported. Japan, Hong Kong, Malaysia, Australia, and Thailand buy most of the oil, but some is retained to fuel power stations and local transport.

Gas production and sales

There are various industrial estates located all over the island. These cater to both heavy and light industries.

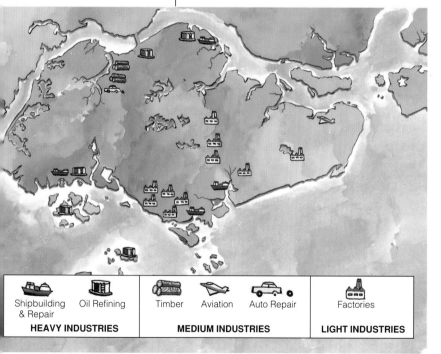

Shipbuilding & Repair	Oil Refining	Timber	Aviation	Auto Repair	Factories
HEAVY INDUSTRIES		**MEDIUM INDUSTRIES**			**LIGHT INDUSTRIES**

Left: **Jurong Industrial Port services Jurong Industrial Town, one of Asia's largest industrial estates. The port can handle almost any type of cargo, from agricultural produce to building materials and steel products.**

Below: **There is no shortage of skilled workers to handle the highly specialized equipment used by most factories.**

have increased in recent years, and a new gas pipeline from Malaysia was opened in 1992.

The manufacturing sector is the mainstay of the economy, especially in electronics. Its industries include the manufacture of color televisions, calculators, radio and cassette recorders, computers, and electronic medical instruments.

In the past there was no choice but to produce low-value goods. The presence of international companies meant higher qualitygoods could be produced and exported. This shifted the emphasis to high-technology, high-value products such as aircraft components and oil-rig construction.

Light industries include food processing, clothing, and the manufacture of household utensils, most of which is carried out in industrial estates.

The garland-maker is an important part of Indian life as he provides the flower garlands needed for Hindu ceremonies and temples.

COTTAGE INDUSTRIES

Few of the cottage industries of old Singapore survive, and it is only a matter of time before they disappear forever. The business problems of the Indian garland-maker are typical: demand for the garlands exists, but mechanization cannot help and no one is willing to do such repetitive daily work for so many hours.

The starting pay, often with lodging and food included, compares well with that offered elsewhere, but young people are uninterested in keeping up a tradition that offers no recognition or opportunity for progress. They prefer to train for something more professional.

The man who wheels a trolley full of homemade festival masks and the woman who designs and sews patchwork quilts are growing old and there is no one to pass their skills to. Some trades like pottery or joss-stick-making involve whole families who have passed on the tradition for generations. But most younger people prefer to work in air-conditioned offices.

HOW THE DRAGON BREATHES

Opening or "dragon head" where firewood is fed in to fire the pots

Holes or "eyes" where more firewood can be fed into the kiln to keep the fire going

Smoke escapes through the chimney

Kiln is built slightly below ground level

Entrances to the kiln which are sealed during firing

Clay pots and vases are stacked inside kiln

THE DRAGON KILN

Chua Eng Cheow built the dragon kiln himself when he and his family came to Singapore from southern China in 1936. Each member has a particular skill that is centuries old, and many of their tasks are still not automated. The family specializes in handmade flower pots, 80% of which go abroad to Australia and Europe.

The kiln is referred to as a "dragon" because of its shape—a long brick structure measuring approximately 138 feet with a chimney at the tail end and a fire box at the dragon's "head." Pots are stacked in huge amounts in the kiln. Then the doorways are sealed, and in the head a fire is lit, which must burn for 18 hours. The rest of the firing is done by stoking through small holes along the body of the dragon. Amazingly, the changes in temperature inside the wood-fired kiln are visually assessed by the men as the color of the flame changes.

However, modern technology and urbanization in Singapore now have resulted in no need for these traditional ways of pottery-making, and the future of the dragon kiln is uncertain.

SOURCES OF REVENUE

Singapore is an entrepot port, which means that imported goods such as printed circuits or telecommunications apparatus are re-exported to other countries. Other exports are goods manufactured in Singapore for sale overseas, including office machines, radio and television receivers, computers, and electronic components. Almost three-quarters of the clothing made in Singapore is exported.

Singapore has the busiest port in the world, coping efficiently with huge amounts of ocean traffic and cargo, 24 hours a day. It is a major port

for passenger liners plying to and from Australia, Europe, the United States, India, and Hong Kong; a destination for oil tankers from the Middle East; and a docking station for ships in need of repair.

Above: **Changi International Airport, with its connections to all major cities, is among the busiest and most efficient in the world. A third terminal is currently being built and land reclamation should lead to a fourth in operation shortly after the turn of the century.**

Right: **The Port of Singapore Authority manages the busiest port in the world at five separate terminals around the island. These deal with computerized container handling, servicing berthed ships, shipbuilding, loading and off-loading cargo, cargo storage, container vessels, and passenger liners.**

WORK ETHIC

Singapore's progress owes much to its work ethic, a striving for excellence with money as motivation and personal success as the goal. But in some areas, concern has been expressed about high staff turnover.

Singaporeans work long hours, driven hard by a government and education system that expects them to excel. Today's workers are better-educated and better-trained, and are therefore more assertive than their predecessors. The growing competitive environment among employers may create even better conditions for local workers. Increasingly, Singapore companies are looking for markets in other countries, and a move has been made to encourage managers and experts to spend time overseas.

NATIONAL CAMPAIGN TO IMPROVE PRODUCTIVITY

In 1972, the National Productivity Board was established to ensure quality and productivity at work. This was followed closely by the Skills Development Fund to provide incentives for employers to fund the training of workers.

A poster used in the productivity campaign

In 1982, an annual productivity campaign was launched with the productivity slogan, "Be The Best That We Can Be." The board's productivity campaigns since 1992 have been guided by the theme of "Quality Work, Quality Life," emphasizing how efficiency and productivity can bring rewards for everyone.

SINGAPOREANS

BY THE TIME OF RAFFLES, a small number of Malays and Chinese had already arrived in Singapore from nearby settlements ruled by the Dutch. The Malays were followed by the Javanese, Bugis, and Balinese from Indonesia, people with a similar lifestyle who were mainly traders and integrated well with the Malays.

The few Chinese worked on gambier and pepper plantations, but the opening up of trading opportunities brought a huge influx of people from different parts of China. Most were laborers and craftspeople who specialized in certain trades. These made up Singapore's four main Chinese dialect groups—the Hokkiens, Teochews, Cantonese, and Hakkas—that settled in separate districts of Chinatown on the south bank of the Singapore River.

Opportunities for work as clerks, technicians, teachers, merchants, and moneylenders brought Indian immigrants from Malaysia, India, and Sri Lanka. In the early 19th century, Singapore became a penal colony for Indian convicts whose labor was needed to build public housing and what were to become Singapore's finest churches and temples. The British also brought in laborers under contract for certain periods to build roads, railways, bridges, and waterways.

The first census, in 1824, claimed a population of 11,000. By 1871 the population had risen to 97,000, and by 1900 to 228,000.

Opposite: **Singporeans at a hawker center indulging in what has been called the national pastime: eating.**

Below: **Routes the various immigrants took to Singapore**

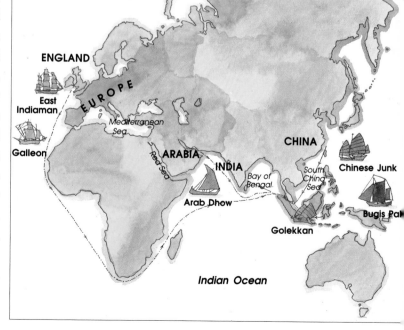

MAIN ETHNIC GROUPS

By 1860 three-fourths of the population was Chinese, followed by Indians, Malays, Arabs, Jews, Eurasians, and Europeans. Even then the society was multicultural, but made up almost entirely of men. Toward the end of the century, women were encouraged to join them, after which many of the immigrants chose to settle in Singapore permanently.

THE CHINESE The first Chinese settlement as designated by Raffles was Chinatown, a large area south of the Singapore River. Chinatown itself was further divided into separate areas for the different dialect-speaking groups, each with a headman to prevent fighting among themselves.

The Chinese who originally settled in Singapore were migrants coming in search of a new life, poor people who were prepared to work very hard to make their fortune. Although those born and bred in Singapore today may feel no ties to a homeland they have never seen, many still hold fast to the work ethic brought over by their forefathers. Despite Westernization, there has been a real effort to retain traditional values.

THE PERANAKAN PEOPLE

Many of the early Chinese emigrants to Malaya and Singapore married Malay women. The result was a separate community of people referred to as the Straits-born Chinese, or "Peranakan," ("per-ran-nah-kan"), which means "locally born."

The Peranakans considered themselves very different from the true Chinese, developing their own unique Peranakan culture. After many centuries they evolved a language of their own, Baba Malay, a mixture of Malay and the Chinese dialect, Hokkien. At the same time, they were one of the first groups of people in the area to begin learning English and to pick up Western customs.

Sadly, the Peranakan people have now vanished as a community and those few remaining are being absorbed into the wider population. However, their unique cuisine lives on in the region—along with their very colorful ceramics, beadwork, and silverware.

Left: **A 19th-century Peranakan family**

Below: **A Malay girl greeting her grandfather in the traditional way. The Malays have remained a very close-knit community despite urbanization.**

THE MALAYS They are the second largest ethnic group and possibly Singapore's original inhabitants. Of the early settlers, the Bugis, former pirates from Sulawesi; the Boyanese from Madura in Indonesia; and the Orang Laut descendants of sea gypsies, have all been absorbed into the Malay culture.

The Malays are a warm and hospitable people united by a common faith, Islam, that pervades their lives. They have now evolved as a group from conservative family life in fishing villages to city life. Separated from the large Malay communities that extend from the Philippines to Thailand, they are developing their own identity as Singaporeans.

A sari shop on Serangoon Road—the "Little India" of Singapore. This was once the area of the original Tamil migrants. Today, it is a street of prewar houses and shops interspersed with temples. Although many Indian families have moved out of "Little India," the area continues to be associated with Indians. A conservation project has started with the intention of improving the older buildings in the area.

THE INDIANS These immigrants originally considered Singapore a temporary base just to make money to send home. They later brought their families and settled down permanently.

Tamils from South India make up about 80% of the whole Indian population, but there are also people from other parts of the Indian subcontinent living in Singapore. These include Gujaratis, Punjabis, Bengalis, Sindhis, Sri Lankan Tamils, and Sinhalese. Perhaps because of their now fading links with India, Singaporean Indians are a close community, careful to preserve their old customs among the variety of cultural influences surrounding them.

THE EURASIANS This is an important minority group mainly of Asian and Portuguese origin from Goa and Malacca. They settled more easily in Singapore, as intermarriage has always been socially acceptable.

NAMES

Chinese people usually have two "given" names and a "family" name, which is placed first. If a man is called Lim See Teo, he is known as Mr. Lim. His wife will retain her father's family name, although she will still be known as Mrs. Lim. Many Singaporeans, those of Chinese origin in particular, also adopt a Western name, either because they become Christians, or because they associate Western names with being more modern.

Malay family names do not last more than one generation. They just add their father's name to the end of their own name. Mr. Jaafar Abdullah may be called Jaafar or Mr. Jaafar. Abdullah is his father's name. His son, Ahmad, will be known as Ahmad Jaafar or Ahmad bin Jaafar. *Bin* or *binte*, meaning "son of" or "daughter of," respectively, may be included between these names but is often dropped these days.

Tamil Singaporeans do not have family names either. They use the initial of their father's name placed before their own; for example, S. Ramasamy, or they use it as a surname, as in Ramasamy Suppiah. An Indian woman will not use her father's name when she gets married but will become simply Mrs. Ramasamy.

All the ethnic groups have separate titles for each family relationship. Children in the United States use the same word, *grandfather*, to refer to their father's or mother's father. In Singapore, the term will vary depending on whose father it is—the mother's father or the father's father. This distinguishes each person from others in the same family and between families.

Aunty and *uncle* are polite forms of address used often by children for any adult who is not a relation. Even vendors at a market stall may use it to communicate with a customer they do not know.

COSTUME

With a few exceptions, Singaporeans wear Western-style dress when they are at work. Other everyday clothes tend to be Eastern or Western depending on how traditional the wearer prefers to be.

Traditional dress usually comes into its own only for special occasions. The Chinese *cheongsam* ("chee-ohng-sahm") is still worn during the Chinese New Year but is otherwise rarely seen except on waitresses in hotel lounges.

Malay women still wear the traditional *baju kurung* ("bah-joo koo-rohng"), a long-sleeved loose blouse worn over an ankle-length skirt, known as a *sarung* ("sah-rohng"). Indians dress in traditional costume mainly for social occasions such as weddings and when going to the temple. The *sari* ("sah-ree"), six yards of material attractively draped around the body, is most commonly worn by women. Men are less likely to be seen in their traditional clothes except at their own weddings or for festive occasions.

Above: **Young Indian women in *saris* at a temple.**

Right: **Malay boys getting dressed in their traditional costume of *baju Melayu* ("bah-joo meh-lah-you")—trousers and shirt with a short piece of material wrapped skirtlike around the waist and tied in front. The hat used is called a *songkok* ("sewng-kohk"). The boy's mother is wearing the *baju kurung.***

Goldsmith shops selling traditional and modern jewelry can be found all over the island.

IMPORTANCE OF GOLD

Gold is highly valued by each of the ethnic groups for both social and financial reasons. As a precious metal, it is considered a worthwhile investment because of its stable property, particularly the more yellow Asian type that has a higher content of gold. For the Chinese, gold jewelry is a special gift for parents to give their daughter when she gets married, a way of wishing her a good marriage and prosperous life.

Malays buy gold as an investment and for luck. Its importance is seen in the *bunga mas* ("boong-eh mahs"), a golden tree that forms one of the ritual aspects of a Malay wedding. It used to be made of real gold, but now gold-colored foil is used instead.

Among Indians, even babies will own a simple gold chain or anklet, and every girl has gold bangles, a gift from her parents that she will wear when she is married.

LIFESTYLE

AFTER TWO DECADES OF STRUGGLE, Singaporeans now see themselves as a cosmopolitan people in touch with new ideas and technologies, well on their way to forging a "city of excellence." To some extent success is taken for granted, and the constraints of the past forgotten. The modern nation has shaped a new forward-looking society that still preserves its traditional values.

The Chinese, Malay, and Indian cultures may seem very different, but they share similar values. The Chinese belief in Confucianism, the Malay *adat* ("ah-daht"), or rules for living, and the Indian traditions all place the family and loyalty to the nation above all else. The government is anxious to emphasize such commonalities so that Singaporeans do not see themselves as disparate races.

Opposite: **Most Singaporeans live in modern high-rise apartment blocks in satellite new towns around the island.**

Below: **Spectators at the National Day Parade—one occasion when Singaporeans show their loyalty and pride to the young nation.**

SOCIAL INTERACTION

Community spirit is considered very important and is fostered by Residents' Committees in public housing estates. The committees arrange a wide range of activities and services and involve themselves in community projects.

The policy is to foster racial harmony, beginning with the housing estates, where 80% of Singaporeans from different backgrounds live together and need to understand each other better.

The post-war baby boom will cause a rise in the number of old people for whom services will be required in the near future. With this in mind, a senior citizens' program is being developed to keep the elderly part of the community for as long as possible.

CIVIL DEFENSE

The aim of the Civil Defense plan is to prepare as many people as possible for a national crisis. Thousands of trained volunteers form closely-knit units that conduct emergency exercises such as food, water and fuel distribution, or blood grouping and collection. This is done in every constituency at regular intervals to familiarize people with emergency plans and procedures.

The program brings everyone who is not eligible for national service—youths, women, and senior citizens—to a better understanding of the need for readiness in peacetime. Various means are used: talks, mobile exhibitions, films, posters, competitions, and mock events are staged.

Civil Defense is just one of five avenues—the others being psychological, social, economic, and military defense—introduced in 1984, which together make up "Total Defense."

FAMILY

More than 80% of Singaporeans live in HDB flats, high-rise apartments in public housing estates managed by the Housing and Development Board. A small minority live in private condominiums and houses.

The resettlement of the population from their traditional lifestyle in the city and coastal areas to the new towns caused a very important social change—the breakup of the extended family. There is no longer the space for grandparents, parents, children, and other relatives to live together. Today about 78% of families in Singapore are nuclear families consisting of parents and children only.

Central to the preservation of the traditional family is filial piety, the lifelong obligation of children to their parents above everyone else. In the past, this entailed total obedience; it has now been simplified by some to mean their duty to return the investment made in them.

Other social and economic changes are rapidly taking their toll on the family. An increase in divorce, working women, and career involvement, and a fall in the birth rate were all major concerns that created a need for counseling services for families having problems. Meanwhile advertising campaigns have been launched emphasizing the more attractive aspects of family life, and in recent years couples have been encouraged to have more children.

A typical nuclear family—father, mother, and two children—in the living room of an HDB flat

CHILDREN

Parents no longer expect their children to be quiet and completely obedient. Modern ideas of education and parenting are very child-centered and may account for the extra attention Singaporean children are given. Ballet and piano lessons after school, at one time out of the reach of most parents, are now common.

Once grandparents were very important caretakers who would tell children stories and pass on values in this way. But now families live in different housing estates, grandparents often work as well as parents, and children spend less time with relatives. Neighbors may look after the children occasionally, or an arrangement is made with a "nanny," usually a woman living nearby, who will mind the children on a full-time basis for a fee. However, the nanny is now being replaced by child-care centers as more women join the work force.

Schools are very exam-oriented, and there is a lot of pressure on children to study hard and do well. Even at the primary level, there are regular tests, as well as mid-year and year-end examinations to keep standards high. After six to eight years of primary school, students move on to secondary school where they spend four to five years depending on their ability. Successful secondary school students can then go on to a two-year or three-year preuniversity course as preparation for university study. Others leave and go to technical colleges for vocational training.

Right: **Besides a hectic school day, many children also attend extra classes for art, music, and dance. A common pastime on weekends is taking part in art competitions like this one.**

Opposite above: **Some families employ an** *amah* **("ah-mah"), or maid, normally a Sri Lankan or Filipina, who will do the housework, some cooking, and babysitting.**

Opposite below: **The** *samsui* **("sahm-swee") women (***samsui* **means "three rivers") were among the first women to come to Singapore in the 1930s. In their distinctive dark blue** *samfoo* **("sahm-foo"), a loose pant suit, and folded red hat, they worked as skilled manual laborers in the building trade.**

WOMEN

After the country's independence, free education up to the secondary level for girls as well as boys was coupled with the need for a larger educated work force. Women were not only able but were actively encouraged to make the best use of their education because it was their parents' investment in future prosperity. At the same time, they were expected to fulfill the traditional role of wife and mother. The modern age has presented women with the challenge of managing both, rather than allowing a choice between one or the other.

Their dilemma is made worse by government pressure on women to marry early, have children, as well as contribute to the work force. Financial help and child-care centers for women returning to work are pitted against the trend of women marrying later than ever before. Many financially independent women enjoy their working life and are in no hurry to marry.

For many of them, busy careers present few opportunities to meet people socially. They also have higher expectations of their life-partners. However, most women still do not expect their husbands to cook and clean. This is because women are more conservatively brought up and still consider themselves responsible for passing on traditions and customs to the next generation.

BIRTH

A dramatic fall in the birth rate in modern Singapore has changed the family planning policy of "Girl or Boy—Two is Enough" to "Have Three Or More If You Can Afford It." Almost overnight in the late 1980s, advertisers and government departments had to switch from making larger families seem unattractive to making them seem a normal aspect of life. Illustrations in school textbooks suddenly had to be revised to conform to the change in government policy, and Singapore television no longer ran advertisements showing mothers being worn down by screaming children.

The government has offered various financial and tax incentives to parents to encourage them to have more children, including a removal of the policy which discriminated against third or fourth children when it came to admission to good schools. The government continues to favor mothers who have university degrees.

It goes without saying that—regardless of government incentives—birth has always been a very important social event in Singapore. This is especially true when a boy is born. Asians traditionally believe that they need a son to carry on the family name or business and to take care of them when they are old. Though women in Singapore have more freedom than in many Asian societies, the delight a male child brings is still deeply ingrained.

Ethnic practices regarding birth vary, depending on how traditional the family is and the degree to which it is influenced by elders. Many young families of all ethnic backgrounds are beginning to break away from elaborate rituals if they are too expensive or impractical, but a celebratory feast or symbolic prayer ritual at the very least is still common.

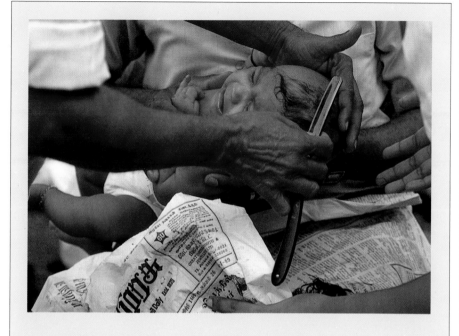

An Indian baby having its head shaved during its first lunar month birth ceremony

ETHNIC PRACTICES REGARDING BIRTH

Nonreligious beliefs and superstitions are common. The new mother is expected to observe certain taboos such as avoiding foods that sap vitality. For at least a month after her baby is born, she is considered "unclean" and must rest at home. During this time she is richly pampered with special foods and tonics to build up her strength.

After a Chinese baby is born, the child's first month day (according to the lunar calendar) is celebrated. The baby, usually dressed in the lucky color red, is shown off to relatives, while red-colored hard-boiled eggs are distributed as symbols of life and energy. Horoscopes may be consulted for a name that will identify the child as having been born in a certain year or generation.

After a Malay baby's first bath, its father recites a Muslim prayer call into its ear to make sure the child grows up a good Muslim. A ritual shaving of its hair is done a week later, after which a feast is held and the baby is given a name from the Koran.

For the Hindus, a priest chooses the first letter of the baby's name and on the 28th day (a lunar month), the child's head is shaved as a thanksgiving. Baby girls may also have their ears pierced at this time

PUBERTY

There is little in the way of rites of passage for Singaporeans, as traditional "growing-up" ceremonies are not always observed. Malay boys are still circumcised at or before puberty, while some Indians have puberty celebrations for girls to wish them a happy married life in the future. The Chinese do not have puberty rituals in their culture.

For all Singaporean boys, National Service is their acceptance into manhood. Since 1967 all male citizens aged 18 or older are expected to serve two-and-a-half years full-time National Service. Most go into the armed forces, but some join the police or the Civil Defense Force. After this, they become reservists, who form 80% of the army. Reservists may be called up at any time, so they must sharpen their skills during compulsory in-camp training each year.

Singapore has found that a civilian army is a useful and less expensive way of maintaining an adequate defense force. It also plays an important part in the mental and physical maturation of young Singaporean men. The bonds they form with colleagues of different social and cultural backgrounds and the military skills they learn equip them to be better workers in civilian life.

Young men and women enjoy spending study or leisure time together. They meet in groups in shopping centers and fast-food restaurants. A generation ago, adults would have been scandalized to see young men and women together unchaperoned. Today it is common to see couples spending time together, hand in hand.

Dating in the Western sense is a fairly recent

All Singaporean males will perform National Service, a rite of passage that cuts across all ethnic groups.

Despite their good fortune, young people face a lot of social pressure. They are caught between old and new Singapore and face confusion over the mix of values in their society. They are expected to study hard and progress in a technological society while remaining loyal to their traditional culture.

occurrence. Young people have been influenced by the mass media and especially by the notion of romantic love, which often conflicts with the more conservative values of their society.

Peer-group pressure is especially strong with the rise of popular culture. Most teenagers are provided with pocket money and additional money may be earned by working in fast-food chains and shopping centers or by tutoring during school vacations. This results in young people with the spending power of adults without adult expenses, giving rise to fears of a pampered materialistic generation with unrealistic expectations for the future.

MARRIAGE AND DIVORCE

Arranged marriages are still common, particularly among the Indians and Malays. For these, the traditional services of a matchmaker may still be called upon. Her role is not as extensive as it was in the past, but the matchmaker may pass on information about a potential bride or groom and arrange meetings between families. Matched couples are often very happy to rely on their parents to choose their future spouses.

The usual practice in Singapore is for couples to take part in a civil ceremony at the Registry of Marriages. This is essential if they are to be eligible for a public housing apartment, even though it could be several years before they get the one they want. Until that time, most couples live apart. Religious rites and family celebrations are postponed until the flat is acquired and furnished and enough money is saved for a customary marriage celebration.

Getting married is an expensive affair, so some young couples choose to participate in mass wedding ceremonies that usually include a dinner and an overseas honeymoon.

GOVERNMENT MATCHMAKERS

The Social Development Unit (SDU) is a modern matchmaking service that encourages male and female graduates to meet, enjoy each other's company during arranged activities, and hopefully consider marriage. In this government-run project, the emphasis is not just on marriage but on quality marriages between couples of equal education.

A second, related project is the formation of Social Development Clubs. These have been set up throughout Singapore to organize activities among single nongraduates for the same purpose. The idea took some time to be accepted, but the formation of the SDU in 1985 has led to many happy marriages.

The Chinese may observe their traditional tea ceremony. As a sign of respect to their family elders, newlyweds serve them tea in order of seniority. There may also be a lavish feast, which often uses up much of the couple's savings.

While the rituals themselves take different forms, the Western white wedding dress is very popular among couples. On Sundays and public holidays, parks are turned into open-air photographic studios where local brides parade in the latest fashions from Paris and New York.

The bride and groom serving tea to the bride's parents during the traditional Chinese tea ceremony. This ceremony initiates the couple into the family and establishes their position within it.

The bridegroom signing the wedding register during the solemnization of a Muslim wedding. The man on the left is officiating at the ceremony.

Malays are married under Muslim law with a traditionally elaborate ceremony. This is usually a very public affair announced by a pair of poles topped with sprays of colored paper twisted around wooden spikes. This is called the *bunga manggar* ("boong-eh mahng-gahr") and depicts a mango tree in bloom to wish the couple many children.

The couple do not live together until after the *bersanding* ("ber-sahn-ding"), when the bride and groom are placed on a raised platform in front of the guests and treated as king and queen. Everyone then takes part in a *kenduri* ("ken-doo-ree"), or celebratory feast.

Hindu wedding ceremonies are a series of symbolic rituals carried out in a temple. The most significant is when the groom ties the *thali* ("tha-lee"), a gold pendant, around the bride's neck to symbolize their marriage. Traditional dowries are still paid, although these are not as large as in the past.

A Hindu bride and groom being blessed at the end of their wedding ceremony

Interracial marriages are not uncommon because many couples think of themselves as Singaporeans rather than belonging to different races.

Divorce in Singapore is on the rise, mainly among the Chinese, followed by the Malays. It is low among Indians because the role of a married person is very important in their culture and gives the women status among friends and relatives.

Muslims are governed by their own laws in matters such as marriage and divorce. A Muslim woman can ask for divorce from her husband if he fails to support her or treats her badly; a Muslim man is allowed up to four wives at a time. However, marriage by Singapore law is monogamous for non-Muslims, unlike in the past when Chinese men could have several wives.

At Chinese funerals, paper offerings, which now include paper representations of credit cards, microwave ovens, and video recorders, are burned to ensure the care of the dead person in the afterlife.

DEATH

Most aspects of life in Singapore are being modernized. Funerals are no exception. At some Chinese funerals, it is not unusual to see the dead person in Western-style dress instead of layers of clothes specially prepared for the occasion. Western bands often take the place of the more somber Chinese musicians, and elaborately decorated truck-hearses are being replaced by glass-sided hearses. These are little more than outward differences because the religious beliefs behind the old rituals remain unchanged. Mourning still lasts the customary 49 days, by which time the dead person is believed to have been reincarnated. The complexity of the rituals varies according to a family's financial situation and preferences, but even the simplest funeral is generally expensive. After the ritual, the body is cremated and the ashes placed in an urn in a columbarium.

A Muslim cemetery

Muslim religious beliefs do not allow for cremation. A pair of vertical stones at the head and foot of the grave are embedded in soil or cemented onto slabs. Rounded headstones are used for men and flat ones for women. Muslims believe they will be reunited with Allah, God, while Hindus believe they will be reborn to make amends for their past sins. For Hindus, the funeral ceremony is usually held at home, after which the body is cremated at a crematorium and the ashes thrown into the sea.

RELIGION

SINGAPORE is a secular state where freedom of worship is offered to everyone. Religion and race are closely bound and people of different faiths respect and tolerate each other's beliefs.

MAIN RELIGIONS

TAOISM When Chinese immigrants first came to Singapore in the 19th century, Chinese Buddhism had absorbed many Taoist beliefs and customs. The distinction between the two philosophies became blurred, so that many people practiced varying combinations of the two.

Taoism is a very old belief system. It began with the teachings of Lao-tzu, a Chinese sage who believed in *Tao* ("The Way"), a path by which people could live in harmony with nature. Centuries later it began to be associated with geomancy, astrology, and magic and later still with Confucian ethics. Its followers in Singapore are mainly the older and less educated Chinese who cling to their folk traditions to prevent feelings of alienation in a rapidly changing society.

CONFUCIUS AND HIS PHILOSOPHY OF LIFE

Kung Fu-tzu was a learned man who held a high position in the Chinese court in the fifth century. He became known as Confucius when a Jesuit priest in China translated his name as such into Latin. His philosophy, Confucianism, is a system of moral ethics that, aside from the main religions, formed the basis of society, education, and administration in China until the 20th century.

In a migrant society like Singapore, Confucianism remains popular with the Chinese because it stresses the importance of keeping ancient traditions alive and fills an emotional void left by the other beliefs, whose concerns are with the spiritual rather than the temporal world.

Top: **Chinese Buddhist monks performing a temple ritual.**

Bottom: **Muslim men at prayer in a mosque.**

BUDDHISM This religion stems from the philosophy of Buddha, an Indian prince who gave up a life of luxury to search for a way to transcend suffering. After years of sacrifice he was "enlightened" and achieved perfect wisdom. This is said to be possible only by following various "noble" paths with the aim of eliminating all human desires.

Most Singaporean Buddhists are Chinese and follow the Mahayana tradition of Buddhism, where merit is gained through good works. The smaller, more monastic, Theravada tradition from Sri Lanka and Thailand has also established temples in Singapore. The two traditions have been brought closer together by programs to promote Buddhism through literature, public talks, and classes as well as social services.

ISLAM The religion of the Malays is Islam, brought to Southeast Asia in the 12th century by Indian and Arab traders. The founder of Islam was the Prophet Mohammed, and his followers are called Muslims. They believe in one God, Allah, and follow a set of beliefs referred to as the Five Pillars of Wisdom that are laid out in their holy book, the Koran.

In Singapore almost all Malays are Muslims, as well as some Indians and Chinese. Religious practice is very much a part of their private and social lives, and they are reminded of their duties daily by a call to prayer, broadcast over the radio or from the mosque, the Muslim place of worship.

HINDUISM This is a religion that reasons that all faiths are simply different paths to the same God. A Hindu believes that living things have souls that are reborn after death, and that people's conduct in the present will have a direct effect on what becomes of them in the future. Almost all Hindus in Singapore are Indian.

The Indians, like the other ethnic groups, brought their religion with them and built temples on various parts of the island. Hinduism once pervaded all of Southeast Asia but lost its hold since, unlike Islam, it is not a missionary religion. Singaporean Hindus, because they are a minority, are a devout group and even maintain some religious customs that have almost died out in India.

For the Hindu, every stage of life is marked by a ritual in which temple worship plays an active part. Most Hindus, whatever their age, will visit their temple at least once a week, and the temple is a focal point during festivals. Priests are still much in demand to perform traditional ceremonies and are brought over from India on two-year contracts to live in the temples.

CHRISTIANITY There is a growing number of Christians in Singapore, and the increase is greater for Protestants than Catholics. More than half of these Christians are converts, mainly English-educated Chinese. This is attributed to a general dissatisfaction with traditional religions and a search for an alternative that is believed to be more modern and rational.

PLACES OF WORSHIP

Early Chinese and Indian temples are among the oldest buildings in Singapore, with some being preserved as national monuments.

In Chinese temples deities are displayed in niches or on altars with the most important deity in the center. Hindu temples are always dedicated to one of the Hindu trinity—the gods of creation, preservation, and destruction—who can be worshiped through any one of a number of attendant deities.

When the Chinese first arrived in Singapore, several places of worship were established by the different migrant groups. Many of these temples still exist.

Muslims must pray five times a day wherever they are and do not worship any images at all. In the mosque, prayers are held under the direction of a religious leader, the *imam* ("i-mahm"). Groups of men meet for daily prayers and special rituals, but women worshipers are not permitted to mix with them. In the evenings, the mosque is used to teach children to read the Koran. Mosques are full of worshipers on Friday, the most important day of the week for Muslims.

With the growth in Christianity there has been a parallel growth in Christian churches, with some groups taking over buildings erected for other purposes and turning them into places of worship.

TEMPLE AND MOSQUE ARCHITECTURE

Chinese temples are arranged in a series of squares with the central one housing the main temple god. They usually face south on elevated ground, according to strict geomantic rules. Huge wooden beams and elaborately decorated pillars support the roof, which usually tilts upward at each end. This is decorated with glazed tiles supporting porcelain gods and symbolic creatures such as the dragon, which brings luck, longevity, or wisdom.

There is no set pattern to the way Hindu temples are built. Most have shrines containing deities, the main one facing east in line with the open door; a hall for worshipers; and an elaborately decorated tower called a *gopuram*. This used to be for distant pilgrims to pray to when they could not go to the temple.

Mosques range from the traditional to the ultramodern. All of them have large courtyards where worshipers can prostrate themselves; an area for ritual washing before prayer; and a minaret, a tower from which loudspeakers call Muslims to prayer. Mosques are decorated with carved geometrical designs and plant motifs as well as Arabic calligraphy, an essential part of Islamic art.

All public housing estates have mosques for their Muslim residents. These are meeting places for organizing various religious projects and celebrating religious ceremonies.

HOLY SYMBOLS

Abstract thought is often represented by symbols. The main religions of Singapore have symbols that convey their special doctrine or philosophy.

THE EIGHT TRIGRAMS These are an arrangement of occult signs consisting of various combinations of straight lines within a circle. The continuous line is a symbol of the male, or *yang* principle, and the broken line is the symbol of the female, or *yin* principle (see box on page 67). The pattern in the center represents harmony in the universe, a perfect balance between *yin* and *yang*. A plaque engraved or painted with the eight trigrams is considered to have the power to protect a home from misfortune and can often be seen hanging over doorways.

THE KORAN The Muslim holy book is renowned as a fine piece of literature. For Muslims, it is a record of the word of Allah as it was given to the Prophet Mohammed by the angel Gabriel. Except at the very beginning, and in a few passages when the Prophet or the angel speaks, the speaker is believed to be God, or Allah himself, which is why the book is of great importance and its word never doubted.

OM The words and syllables of the holy *Vedas*, ancient Indian scriptures, have always been revered by Hindus, and certain syllables are believed to be particularly holy. The word *om* ("ohm") is said to contain the essence of the *Vedas*, giving it power and mystery.

Among the Hindu Brahmins or priestly sect, the word *om* symbolizes the entire universe. It is repeated during worship and as a sacred utterance during meditation.

The Bodhi tree outside the Sri Lankaramaya Temple. This is believed to be descended from the Bodhi tree under which the Buddha attained enlightenment. However, the most detailed account of events concerning the enlightenment do not mention the Bodhi tree and there does not seem to be any historical evidence of the tree's existence. The worship of sacred trees was a common feature of ancient Indian life and may have been absorbed into Buddhism.

THE BODHI TREE This is an important Buddhist symbol because it was while sitting under this large fig tree that the Buddha attained enlightenment. *Bodhi* ("boh-dhee") is an Indian term that means "awakening." Saplings grown in various monasteries are said to be descended from the original tree under which Buddha sat and are therefore treated as sacred. In Singapore, there is a Bodhi tree outside the Buddhist Sri Lankaramaya Temple's main prayer hall. The tree arrived as a sapling from Sri Lanka.

FOLK BELIEFS

The Chinese are heavily influenced by the supernatural and spend much of their lives appeasing ghosts and ancestors, and consulting mediums when they have failed to do so.

The once-powerful Malay *bomoh* ("boh-moh"), part-healer, part-adviser, is in touch with the spirit world. He offers his services in exorcism or matchmaking for a small donation. Like the Indian medicine man and the Chinese doctor, or *sinseh* ("sin-sayh"), he uses herbs to cure. If these do not work, the *bomoh* relies on magic and incantation.

The Chinese are obsessed with the idea of long life and good health. It is believed that illness is caused by a loss of inner, or *yin/yang,* balance in the body that can be restored by various herbal remedies. This corresponds with the Indian system known as ayurveda, where illness is said to be caused by an imbalance of body fluids. The Malays have a similar faith in *jamu* ("jah-moo"), a herbal mixture, ground and then drunk as a panacea for a variety of ills. Traditional medicine is often preferred to Western medicine because it is inexpensive and research has shown much of it to be reliable—the main difference is that it treats the whole body and not just the part that is ill.

FENG SHUI Modern belief in *feng shui* ("fehng-shway") is a combination of beliefs in *yin* and *yang* and other beliefs in ghosts and ancestor worship. The practice developed from animistic feelings about nature combined with a "science" or set of rules that allows people to live in harmony with nature. It is a system that provides guidelines for siting buildings and graves auspiciously, and is taken very seriously even in modern Singapore.

The *yin-yang* symbol

THE *YIN-YANG* PRINCIPLE

The Chinese believe that the world is made up of *chi* or creative energy, which is responsible for *yin* and *yang*. These are idealized opposites that dominate nature yet remain unnoticed within it, blending with each other in constantly changing amounts. Heaven is *yang,* Earth is *yin*—everything in the universe is contained in these basic forces. *Yang* is positive, active, masculine, and found in everything warm, dry, and bright. *Yin* is negative, passive, feminine, and found in things soft, shady, and secret.

   The Chinese strive to balance these two states to create harmony in their lives. Too much of either creates an imbalance that must be corrected if one is to live happily. This principle is even applied to eating and to illness since the *yin/yang* balance affects the human body both from inside and out.

LANGUAGE

THERE ARE FOUR OFFICIAL LANGUAGES: Malay, the national language; Mandarin, the official language of the majority group; Tamil, the language of 60% of Singapore's Indians; and English, the language of business and administration, which blends these cultures together.

A DIVERSITY OF TONGUES

Most people in Singapore are multilingual, speaking at least one of the local languages and English. Each ethnic majority is encouraged to continue using its "mother tongue," which is a very important vehicle for the transmission of beliefs and values to the next generation.

Although English is often spoken well, a local patois is also used. This is referred to as "Singlish," an amalgam of English, various Chinese dialects, and Malay. It is not grammatical and is spoken with a sing-song accent, the voice lifting at the end of groups of words. For example, "Why so stubborn-lah?" translates to "Why are you being so stubborn?"

SPEAK MANDARIN CAMPAIGN

In a country as small and diverse as Singapore, similarities rather than differences within groups need to be emphasized. In the 1970s, it was noted that dialects were preventing the Chinese from considering themselves a unified group. So a link among these various groups was forged by the adoption of Mandarin, the language of Beijing.

In 1979, a national campaign was mounted, with television advertisements and street slogans, advising citizens to "Speak Mandarin" and less dialects. Mandarin is taught in schools, used on television and radio, and is now spoken increasingly by Chinese Singaporeans. The older generation still feels more comfortable with dialects, but there are many young Singaporeans who do not understand the language of their ancestors.

NONVERBAL LANGUAGE

As thoughts and feelings remain unsaid, physical objects are used as symbols to convey nonverbal messages. For example, an old Chinese couple who are reluctant to show any love for each other may find they can do so through a grandchild.

One very important facet of unexpressed emotion in Singapore is "loss of face," a sensation of inferiority or humiliation, as a result of feeling "exposed" in front of others. For example, a child will not argue with his parents in public for fear of embarrassing his family, and a worker does not question his superiors in case he appears to question their judgment. Thus out of politeness and to save "face," a Singaporean may publicly agree to do something that privately he does not intend to.

Singaporeans may laugh at situations that do not seem funny to a Westerner, and therefore, it is important to distinguish between laughter and humor. Laughter is often a cover for embarrassment, to hide "loss of face."

Nonverbal taboos are shared by each of the ethnic groups. People do not often touch each other physically in public once they are adults. Handshakes are the most common form of greeting across cultures, particularly between men and women, although each group has its own individual style of greeting.

The Malay style of greeting is the Islamic handshake. You hold both hands of the other person, then bring your hands to your chest.

zǐ

子

infant;
child;
son

The character for "child" originated from a representation of an infant with outstretched arms and legs. It was modified to one with legs swaddled in cloth bands. Presumably, to the Chinese parent, the secret of infant care lies in keeping one end wet, and the other dry.

SCRIPT

The Chinese script has remained unchanged for over a thousand years, the characters standing for a combination of sounds and ideas based on simple pictographs. The addition of extra lines or dots to the pictographs suggests closely related ideas, while two or more pictographs are joined to convey abstract ideas. Pictographic combinations can also suggest two items sharing the same sound. In the 1960s in China, the characters were simplified and standardized, and some years later Singapore followed suit. Efforts have also been made to standardize the spelling of Chinese words in English by using a system called Hanyu Pinyin ("Han-yoo Pin-yin").

The earliest Malay script was an alphabet of South Indian origin. Four centuries later it was written in an Arabic script called Jawi. Both the Dutch and the British colonialists transcribed the Arabic symbols into the Roman alphabet. The language used in Singapore has been brought in line with changes made in the neighboring countries of Malaysia and Indonesia.

The script of the Tamil Indians comes from the oldest Dravidian language, used mainly by people living in Tamil Nadu in South India and Sri Lanka. Its basic structure has remained unchanged for almost 2,500 years yet its script has no connection with other Indian scripts. Tamil was one of the earliest languages to develop a rich store of written literature.

How a Chinese character evolves—according to Singaporean writer Peng

ARTS

SINGAPORE has always had a great deal of culture but little chance to make anything of it. Now that more opportunities exist to do so, professionalism is being nurtured.

THEATER AND DRAMA

Cross-cultural influences have added a fresh dimension to well-known works of all ethnic groups. The French opera *Orpheus in the Underworld* and the Indian epic the *Ramayana* have been translated into Mandarin for those who are not able to appreciate them in their original languages.

Chinese street operas have been common in Singapore from the 1940s. Chinese clans and community groups still conduct opera classes and workshops. Performances are usually held during Chinese festivals, and as they are held in honor of the gods, they are always free. Today, classical Chinese opera can also be enjoyed in air-conditioned theaters with large seating capacities, a reflection of their popularity. Locals and tourists who may not understand the language can enjoy these performances since there are English subtitles.

Malay theatrical traditions such as the *bangsawan* (Malay opera) have seen a revival in recent years as a medium for telling dramatic stories. It is important to note that Malay and Indian drama is rarely complete without music and dance.

There are often free performances of *Bharathanatyam*, a form of Indian classical dance, at temples during the Hindu festival of Navra-atri.

DANCE

Apart from the lion dance (see box opposite), other traditional Chinese dances are now rarely performed except at cultural shows for tourists.

Malay dance can be said to be divided into *tarian* ("tah-ree-yan"), or pure dance, and *taridra* ("tah-ree-drah"), or dance-drama, sections. Steps are memorized but not in a serious manner. Neither is the music nor movements for the different Malay dances learned. As a result, even the finest dances are disappearing.

Indian dance is considered an important means of keeping the young in touch with their community and religion. However, few young people are happy to spend the many years necessary to learn ancient Indian art forms. This is especially true of the exacting movements of the *Bharathanatyam,* a traditional South Indian devotional dance.

The Chinese lion dance
in a street parade.

THE CHINESE LION DANCE

To the Chinese, the lion has been synonymous with demon-scaring for centuries. The lion dance did not come to Singapore until 1925, when the first troupe arrived from southern China. The dance was originally associated solely with the Chinese New Year but is now part of any important undertaking. It is accompanied by fierce drumming.

The lion's head with its exaggerated features is a rattan frame decorated in bright colors. It is worn by two men, one crouched behind the other. The impact of the dance, which is intended to show courage, depends upon the coordination of these two performers.

The performers are often martial-arts pupils as the dance is acrobatic and requires much stamina. It takes about a year to learn the steps, but as only skillful dancers are paid for their services, frequent practice is necessary.

The object of the dance is to overcome various obstacles put in the way and reach some green leaves, usually lettuce—the lion's reward for the good fortune its presence has brought. Originally, the cut greens also signified the start of new growth in the fields after the harvest.

A Chinese orchestra performing in a concert hall

MUSIC

Concerts of the Chinese classics are primarily renditions of the *er hu* ("err-hoo") and the *gao hu* (kow-hoo"), both stringed instruments, while other smaller groups offer Chinese choral singing and folk songs.

Groups singing traditional love songs called *ghazal* ("ghah-zahl") used to be an important part of local Malay wedding entertainment in the 1950s and 1960s. A few of these groups remain but now double up as wedding bands playing contemporary music. Another form of song is *dikir barat* ("dee-kir bah-raht"), the choral singing that usually accompanies drama.

Indian music has similar instrumental and vocal traditions, both still heavily influenced by classical forms. In Singapore there are various arts organizations that bring teachers in from India to teach classical music, and performances of both North and South Indian music are held on stage.

The Singapore Symphony Orchestra was formed in 1979. Since then, it has brought music from baroque to 20th-century composers, including regional works, to the local population.

Besides regular concerts, there is also the annual Festival of Music. Over 100 groups, both local and foreign, offer a wide variety of music from jazz and computer music to Chinese, Malay, and Indian traditional music during the two-month-long festival. Some of the performances are held in the open air to bring the music to as many people as possible.

Open-air concerts in the parks are quite common during weekends and public holidays. Whole families enjoy the music provided by school, amateur, and professional bands and orchestras.

MUSIC FOR EVERYONE SERIES

The Music for Everyone series was first begun in the 1960s. The original idea was to subsidize the cost of concerts to encourage more people to attend cultural events.

Now the series encompasses as many varied musical performances as possible within its budget. In the past, a large percentage of foreign musicians were featured, but there is now more emphasis on local musical talent. The concerts have been held at different locations—even in a train station—to make the music more accessible to the people.

ISKANDER JALIL, MODERN POTTER

Iskander Jalil, a highly qualified artist, has been a potter since 1960. His innovative designs, based on Japanese styles and influenced by Islamic calligraphy, have been featured in many exhibitions. His method is to use local materials and retain the earthy quality of the clay rather than to rely on glazes.

He sees himself more as a craftsman than as an artist. In spite of this, he was given a special award for art by the Ministry of Culture in 1975 and awarded the National Cultural Medallion, the highest award in Singapore for the arts, in 1988. He enjoys teaching at his own workshop and at local educational establishments, aiming to give his students a strong base in pottery and to leave something of himself behind.

ART AND ARTIFACTS

The National Museum Art Gallery, housed on one of the upper floors of the National Museum, was established around a gift of some early local works by a Singaporean philanthropist in the 1960s. Since then, many local artists have donated their own work to the collection. Due to restricted space, there are now plans to convert an old school into an art gallery to allow more works of art to be displayed.

The National Museum houses the ethnology, history, and art of Singapore and Southeast Asia, including stone sculptures, traditional

textiles, and ceramics. Although improvements are regularly made, there is always a chronic shortage of space. Large exhibitions are held at other locations such as the Empress Place building, which was once government offices, now remodeled into a museum for traveling Asian art and cultural exhibits.

Art can be seen in many aspects of Singaporean life—on postage stamps, in government offices, and even at train stations, as seen in this picture.

LITERATURE

Singaporeans enjoy a 91.1% literacy rate but rarely read for pleasure. They read mainly to collect information to improve themselves or to pass examinations. Television and magazines are preferred to books because a wide range of subjects can be absorbed in a short time.

However, there is a growing interest in literature. Books dealing with Singaporean subjects almost always become bestsellers at the annual Singapore International Festival of Books, which, from small beginnings, has grown into a large regional book fair.

The development of Singapore's own literature reflects a consciousness of national identity, as local people search for a style of their own. The local flavor of these books appeals to Singaporeans. However, most writers in Singapore cannot make a living from writing and must pursue it in their spare time.

LEISURE

THE MANY OFFSHORE ISLANDS of Singapore are ideal for picnics and snorkeling; a few have camping facilities too. Some Singaporeans like to sunbathe, but most prefer to relax in a shady part of the beach. They swim in artificial sheltered lagoons because the open sea has been polluted by heavy ocean traffic and many areas have a strong undercurrent. Smaller islets and reefs have been merged by land reclamation to provide suitable areas for boating, sailing, scuba diving, sea fishing, and other marine activities.

There are about 38 public parks scattered across the island, each having some particular feature of interest. One new coastal park allows bird life to be observed at close range, while another offers one of the biggest fitness courses with panoramic views over the sea.

City parks provide a number of leisure activities, whether as modern recreation and performance centers or as rejuvenated historical landmarks. Many have reservoirs or lakes and attractive scenery and offer an escape from the city with quiet walks and bird-singing corners.

The east coast of Singapore was, until recently, the refuge of rich island dwellers who lived in large bungalows overlooking the sea. Land reclamation created the East Coast Parkway, the site of fine seafood restaurants, sea sports, camping, barbecues, cycling, and walks along the seafront.

Opposite: **Aerial view of Kusu Island, an offshore island known for its Chinese temple and picnic facilities**

Below: **Windsurfing is an activity that is enjoyed by many young Singaporeans. It is common to see enthusiasts out in full force off the east coast each weekend.**

Spinning tops, or *gasing*, a traditional leisure activity still played today

GAMES

Congkak ("chong-kak"), a traditional Malay game of chance played by adults and children, is one of the many ethnic games now fast disappearing. It requires a long, thin, wooden board with rounded ends, containing two rows of small indentations or "holes" in which beans, peanuts, or marbles are placed. As the game progresses, these gradually accumulate in two larger holes at each end, known as the *congkak* "houses." The person with the most beans, peanuts, or marbles collected there wins.

Gasing ("gah-sing"), or "spinning tops" are traditional toys with which Malays and Chinese still play today. The tops are made of wood in two different sizes, a large top threaded with string that causes it to spin, or a smaller type, that can be spun with the finger and thumb.

Carom ("CARE-rehm"), a game of Indian origin, is very popular in Singapore. Played by two to four players, it is similar to the American game of pool but is much smaller in scale and does not use cues. It consists of a board about 2-feet square with a net pocket at each corner. Counters are pocketed by means of a colored "striker" flicked with the finger and thumb. The object of the game is to remove as many of the opponents' counters from the board as possible.

Mahjong ("mah-johng") is another game that is extremely popular in Singapore. Played with tiles, it is a game of chance originally played by the aristocracy in China. These tiles, now made of plastic rather than ivory as in the past, are engraved with sets of Chinese symbols and characters. The object is to complete a winning hand of certain sets of tiles as quickly as possible, while preventing opponents from doing the same. Neighborhoods come alive with the noise of the "clickity-clackity" sound of the movement of the tiles during weekend *mahjong* parties and the Chinese New Year.

One of the more modern games played in the school playground is Zero Point, popular among girls. A series of elastic bands strung together make a long flexible "rope." One child holds each end, while a third makes skillful maneuvers across the bands as they are raised gradually from ankle to head-height. Skateboarding and cycling stunts with BMX bikes are very popular among boys.

CHINESE CHESS

Chinese chess, or *xiang qi* ("see-ang chee"), is a game of strategy for more intellectual players. Like Western chess, it has 64 squares on the board, but pieces are placed where the lines cross rather than in the squares. It is also separated into two opposing countries in the middle by a "river." Each country, or side, has 16 pieces consisting of various military forces.

Another form of chess is *wei qi* ("way-chee"), sometimes called "Go." In this game, the opponent's pieces are surrounded rather than captured. The game is growing in popularity in community centers because it has few rules yet can be played at many different levels of complexity.

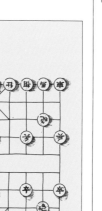

Above: **Skateboarding and BMX bike stunts are very popular with the young. A special park has been constructed so that stunts can be practiced safely.**

Left: **A Chinese chess board.**

SPORTS

Singapore's sports facilities include indoor and outdoor stadiums, tracks, multipurpose playing fields, sports halls, swimming complexes, and a sailing lagoon, as well as outdoor exercise apparatus in public fitness parks. Newly planned facilities include rock climbing on an offshore island and a skateboard park.

One traditional sporting game still played is *sepak raga* ("say-pahk rah-geh"). *Sepak* in Malay means "to kick" while *raga* means "basket," referring to a ball made of woven rattan. The ball, which must not be allowed to touch the ground, is tossed to players of a team using any part of the body but the hands. Until recently, no proper rules existed for the game, but it has now been formalized and is popularly known by its Thai name, *sepak takraw* ("say-pak tahk-raw"), and a more durable, plastic ball is used.

Soccer, rugby, cricket, field hockey, and golf were introduced by the British, and soccer is now considered to be the national sport. During the soccer season, matches for the Malaysia Cup are played at the National Stadium between Singapore and various states of Malaysia. There are no professional teams but a semiprofessional league has just been established, making the game more exciting for its thousands of fans.

Cricket is inevitably linked to the Padang, or "field" where it has been played since the 1820s. The cricket season is from March until September, after which rugby takes over until the following March. Field hockey and tennis are also played on the Padang.

Once considered to be a game for the elderly, golf is now growing in popularity among the island's social elite. Apart from public driving ranges, there is no public course, but one is planned for the future.

Water sports, especially boating and angling, are popular activities on the east coast and, more recently, in the newly cleaned rivers. The World Power-Boat Grand Prix, the International Water Skiing Championships, and the International Dragon Boat Races have been held in Singapore's waters.

Tai-chi ("tie-chee"), or shadow boxing, and *qigong* ("chi-gong") have a large following, especially among the elderly. These are forms of martial art, where passive movements build inner vitality, strengthen the body, and rest the mind.

Joggers are a common sight in the early hours of the morning and late hours of the evening, especially in the parks surrounding the reservoirs.

STORYTELLING

Storytelling is a Chinese tradition that developed as a form of theatrical entertainment, but such traditional forms are dying out in Singapore. In the past, fine storytellers, though often illiterate, would sit under a tree in Chinatown or at Boat Quay, telling a story in the time it took a joss stick to burn. They would then collect payment from the audience. These men have all grown old now, but the tradition lives on in some clan associations.

Although the storytellers drew on well-known tales, they also told entertaining anecdotes to make the stories more exciting. Their traditional role has now been taken over by libraries, and to a lesser extent, by bookshops and television, which hold storytelling sessions with a more modern slant, followed by discussions and activities.

Malays have a great store of folktales told by generations of wandering storytellers. Most of their traditional literature, both prose and poetry, has been kept alive by word of mouth and is an art form widely used to pass on social and moral values.

Sanskrit scripture has passages that use stories for both religious and secular reasons. The *Ramayana,* an epic poem about a much-loved Hindu deity, Rama, has unparalleled popularity in Southeast Asia and is told through dance dramas or at festival times.

Educational and recreational programs are organized by the National Library and its branches. Talks, films, and storytelling sessions for children encourage the use of the library and get parents involved in reading to children. Teachers are also encouraged to read to their students, especially preschoolers, shown here.

VACATION PURSUITS

Seaside retreats on the offshore island of Sentosa offering an overnight stay include vacation chalets, hostels for large groups of young people, or campsites that offer tents, barbecue pits, and camp beds for rent. Those who want to stay closer to home book into chalets along the east coast, or even into local hotels for a spate of uninterrupted luxury.

Day trips, especially over long weekends, are often made over the short causeway into Malaysia by bus, car, or train.

The monorail on Sentosa ("Island of Tranquility"). The most developed resort island, it offers a great variety of leisure pursuits and is an escape from the fast-paced life of the city. It can be reached within a few minutes by bus, ferry, or cable car from the mainland.

Malaysia offers an escape from the hustle and bustle of city life to a more naturally scenic environment. Proof of the popularity of this destination lies in the long lines of cars waiting for immigration formalities at both ends of the causeway.

Twenty years ago, visiting places beyond Malaysia was a luxury available only to the rich. Today most people want to travel to see the world, although taking time off from work to do so is a new idea. Australia, Europe, China, and the United States are favorite destinations. In 1988, Singaporeans made more than 850,000 trips by air, not including the millions of overland trips to Malaysia.

HOBBIES AND PASTIMES

Singaporeans work a five-and-a half-day week, so evenings, and particularly Sundays, are opportunities to unwind and indulge in favorite pastimes. Many of these activities are organized by groups promoting social and recreational events for adults and children.

The People's Association oversees a network of community centers throughout the island that offers a changing list of cultural programs, crafts, and skills.

Karaoke ("kah-rah-oh-kay"), Japanese for "empty orchestra," is a hobby that took Singapore by storm in the 1980s. This is the singing of favorite songs to pretaped music without vocals. Enthusiasts meet at *karaoke* lounges where song lyrics and video images of scenery are provided. At some, singers can see themselves on television monitors and

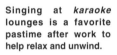
Singing at *karaoke* lounges is a favorite pastime after work to help relax and unwind.

on a big screen.

Kite-flying has been a favorite pastime for centuries and is still common in Singapore. Kites are made from thin, oily paper or cellophane and can be quite elaborate in shape and design. Each year there is a National Kite Flying Festival in which teams from many nations participate.

Other enjoyable pastimes for Singaporeans are two national obsessions: shopping and eating. Singapore has often been referred to as "a shopper's paradise" because of its convenient shopping plazas, long business hours, safety, and duty-free imports. A vast range of commodities means almost anything is available from a fur coat to the newest electronic gadget.

Eating is a social activity enjoyed by all, although lunching out informally is more common than dining together. Restaurants are particularly busy during weekends when the whole family will make this a special trip. Food courts are becoming popular. For people anxious to squeeze in as much pleasure as possible on their days off, these air-conditioned areas in shopping centers serve a range of fast food from Japanese sushi to frozen yogurt.

Layang-layang ("lah-yang lah-yang"), meaning kites in Malay, have been flown for centuries in Southeast Asia. This has been developed into an art, and every February teams from many countries come to compete in the National Kite Flying Festival.

SONGBIRDS

Untrained songbirds are kept by all ethnic groups because they are inexpensive and easily cared for in small apartments. Once only an interest for elderly men, training these songbirds has now become so popular a hobby in modern Singapore that many coffee shops and housing estates include a bird corner equipped with poles and wires to hang cages. Made out of bamboo, these cages are beautifully carved and decorated with ivory ornaments and porcelain bowls.

The first bird-singing competition was held in 1953, just for pleasure. Now owners go to a lot of trouble to train singing birds, which fetch thousands of dollars in prize money. A National Songbird Competition has been held annually since 1982, but many local competitions organized by community centers are held throughout the year.

During the competitions, hundreds of bird cages are hung from poles out in the open. Birds are judged on the basis of their movements, physique, stamina, and singing times.

FESTIVALS

Singapore's ethnic and religious diversity means that its calendar is filled with festivals, bringing additional color and life to an already bustling tropical island.

TAOIST/BUDDHIST FESTIVALS

The Zong, or Dragon Boat Festival is held in remembrance of the death of a famous Chinese poet, Qu Yan, who, in protest against corruption, threw himself into the river Mi Lo in China in 230 B.C. Local fishermen rushed out in their boats to save him, throwing mounds of rice into the water and beating drums to keep hungry fish away. To mark the occasion in Singapore, local and international teams of 22 rowers and a drummer complete a 760-yard race in long fiberglass boats decorated like dragons, each painted with scales and sporting an awesome head and sharp tail.

Qing Ming ("Ching Min") is the festival that is often referred to as the Chinese All-Soul's Day and is an important event for a people who do not believe that family relationships are broken by death. In the old agricultural communities of China, the dead were seen as being able to ensure a good harvest. Now they are seen to benefit families who honor their memory.

The Festival of the Hungry Ghosts stems from the belief that for one month each year, the dead return to earth and must be entertained.

Opposite: **The dragon boat race features international teams each year during the Dragon Boat Festival. Before the boats are launched, they are blessed in a "dotting-the-eye" ceremony to give the boats "vision."**

Below: **During Qing Ming, paper money is burned for the spirits. Food, chopsticks, and paper models of everyday items are placed at the grave to be enjoyed in the afterlife. Grave sites are tidied, joss sticks are lit, and families pay their respects.**

Paper lanterns in traditional shapes of dragons and unicorns as well as modern airplanes appear in the shops about a month before the Mooncake Festival. On the night when the moon is at its brightest, processions of lantern-carrying children can be seen all over the island.

Because of the mischief these ghosts can cause, there are no marriages, family festivities, or important undertakings during this month.

The Mid-Autumn or Mooncake Festival falls in the month when the moon is said to be at its brightest. Chinese Singaporeans observe it as their ancestors would have, with music, family outings, and mooncakes. These are round golden-brown pastries stuffed with a variety of ingredients including beans, lotus seeds, preserved duck eggs, nuts, and minced meats.

The Chinese or Lunar New Year is the best loved Chinese festival. It is also called the Spring Festival because for the agricultural people of China, this was an important time to give thanks for the harvest and pray for the coming year. Today it is a time to review the past and make plans for the future. The reunion dinner on Lunar New Year's Eve is the most important event that all family members are expected to attend.

The color red promises success. It denotes good luck; household objects may be painted red to attract luck. Red clothes are worn for the same reason; a red banner over the door brings luck to those who enter the house; and children receive *hongbao* ("hong-pao"), small red packets containing money for good luck.

Vesak Day marks Buddha's birth, enlightenment, and death according to the Buddhist lunar calendar, and is named after the month it falls in. Buddhists fast on this day, bring flowers and fruit to the temple, listen to the monks chanting, and pray. They are expected to do good deeds ranging from feeding the poor to releasing caged birds.

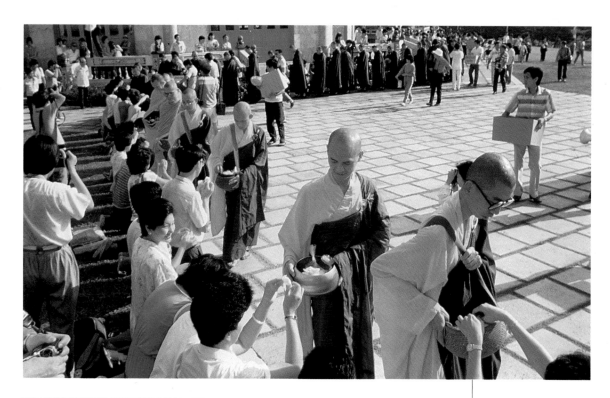

THE CHINESE LUNAR CALENDAR

Ancient Chinese astrologers invented a calendar based on a 60-year cycle—made up of five 12-year cycles—that is still used today. Each of these 12 has the name of an animal to make it easy to remember.

Each year is divided into 6 "large moons" of 30 days and 6 "small moons" of 29 days, based on the moon's movement around the earth. Because the lunar year has 354 days compared with the 365 ¼ days of the solar calendar, they compensated for the difference by adding an extra month to every third year in the 12-year cycle.

Legend has it that Buddha called the animals to him with the object of pairing each of them with a year in the lunar cycle. The first to arrive was the rat, followed by the ox, tiger, rabbit, dragon, snake, horse, goat, monkey, cockerel, dog, and the pig. Thus each cycle begins with the Year of the Rat and ends with the Year of the Pig, and people born in these years are said to take on characteristics of that animal.

Above: **Buddhist devotees giving alms to monks on Vesak Day**

Below: **The Chinese astrological calendar**

MUSLIM FESTIVALS

Hari Raya Puasa, or Hari Raya Aidil Fitri is the biggest celebration in the Muslim calendar. It follows immediately after *Ramadan,* the month of fasting when Muslims do not eat or drink between sunrise and sunset. Fasting is believed to purify the body and soul and is a reminder of the suffering of others.

During the fasting month, shops and markets turn out cakes, sweets, and pastries. Just before the appearance of the new moon, new clothes are bought, houses are cleaned, and people are busy preparing special food for the festivities. It is also common for families to visit cemeteries to tidy grave sites and recite verses from the Muslim holy book, the Koran.

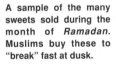

A sample of the many sweets sold during the month of *Ramadan*. Muslims buy these to "break" fast at dusk.

A customary annual ritual is to ask forgiveness from elders for past misdeeds. Children receive money in green packets rather like the Chinese *hongbao,* and all Muslims must contribute an annual *fitrah* ("fit-rah"), a tithe that is used by the Muslim religious council for several purposes, one of which is to help poor students. It is not a tax but a means of giving to others.

A Malay family in their Hari Raya finery

Hari Raya Haji, or Hari Raya Aidil Adha ("Great Day of Sacrifice") marks the period of the *haj,* or annual pilgrimage to Mecca, which falls on the last month of the Muslim calendar, five weeks after the monthlong fasting ends. It is very important for a Muslim to make a trip to the holy city of Mecca at least once in his or her lifetime and join the faithful from other parts of the world.

The trip will earn the male Muslim the title *haji* ("hah-jee") and a woman, *hajjah* ("hah-jah"). Prayers of thanks and ritual animal sacrifices are offered at mosques in memory of Ibraham's (Abraham) willingness to sacrifice his own son in obedience to Allah's will.

THE MUSLIM CALENDAR

The Muslim era dates from the year in which Prophet Mohammed migrated from Mecca to Medina. The first day of the first year was fixed at July 16, A.D. 622. The years of the Muslim calendar are lunar and always consist of 12 lunar months alternately 30 and 29 days long. The year has 354 days, but the last month sometimes has 30 days, making a total of 355 days for that year.

97

HINDU FESTIVALS

Navraatri, or the Festival of Nine Nights, pays homage to the Goddess Shakti in each of her three forms—Parvathi, Lakshmi, and Saraswathi, consorts to the Hindu Trinity. Three days of the festival are allotted to each of them. Each represents a different aspect of God, and any one of them can be worshiped in various personal ways. Their freshly garlanded images are dressed and displayed prominently in temples, offerings are laid before them, and each night performances of classical dance and music are held.

Thaipusam is when, as a form of penance, male Hindu devotees walk barefoot along a two-mile route carrying a heavy steel framework, or *kavadi* ("kah-vah-di"), weighing up to 70 pounds. This is anchored onto their bare flesh with small hooks and adorned with limes, images of gods, small vessels of milk, and peacock feathers.

The practice has its beginnings in a story of a devotee in India struggling under a load to reach Lord Shiva's son, Lord Murugan, who had summoned him. Since then, devotees perform this act as penance or in thanks for a wish granted. Women carry a smaller, half-*kavadi* on their shoulders, but their cheeks and tongues are often similarly pierced.

Thimithi honors the Hindu goddess Draupadi (see box). Over a thousand devotees walk, seemingly oblivious to pain, across a 10-foot-long pit filled with smoldering ash, to give thanks for her help in

THE *MAHABHARATA*

This Indian epic poem narrates the struggle for supremacy between two related families, the Kauravas and the Pandavas. Draupadi is pledged in marriage to the five Pandava brothers, but their jealous cousin Duryodhana challenges the eldest Pandava brother to a game of dice and wins her for himself. When he begins to disrobe her, she is saved from humiliation by Lord Krishna to whom she appeals for help. She curses Duryodhana and swears she will not braid her hair until she can oil it with his blood. When he eventually dies, she performs her grisly task and walks on fire to prove her chastity. Devotees follow her example to prove they have similarly kept an important vow.

A temple decorated for Deepavali, the Hindu Festival of Lights

overcoming problems. In a related ceremony, women devotees circle the temple ground, kneeling in prayer after every third step.

Deepavali, which means "a garland of lights," is the Hindu Festival of Lights. It falls on the night of the new moon and celebrates Lord Krishna's victory over the demon of darkness. In Singapore, electric lights now decorate the streets and houses, taking the place of the traditional oil lamps that were previously used.

Above: **During the Christmas season, hotels and stores in the main shopping area are lit up and decorated.**

Opposite above: **The National Day Parade on August 9 at the National Stadium is the highlight of celebrations to commemorate Singapore's independence.**

Opposite below: **The largest street party of the year, "Swing Singapore" is held at the end of the monthlong National Day celebrations in August.**

CHRISTIAN FESTIVALS

Good Friday is commemorated with night services in churches to mark the occasion of the crucifixion of Christ. At St. Joseph's Church, worshipers carry candles during the evening service to symbolize Christ's light in the world, after which a candle-lit procession emerges from and re-enters the church. Some Christians offer penance by abstaining from meat or fasting on this day.

Christmas is celebrated in the traditional manner with feasting, church-going, and an exchange of cards and gifts. The main shopping area is lit up and decorated, recordings of carols play continuously in the stores, and Santa makes his rounds in his traditional red costume in spite of the heat. The commercial emphasis on Christmas in Singapore allows it to be enjoyed with equal fervor by the entire community.

NONRELIGIOUS CELEBRATIONS

Singaporeans remember their country's beginnings as an independent nation each year in August. The highlight of celebrations is the parade on National Day. A lengthy parade of decorated floats, bands, and dancers makes its way through the city streets either to the Padang, the large grassy area near the seafront, historically the focus of important events, or to the National Stadium. Here military displays and thematic celebrations emphasize the growth of the young nation. At the end of the monthlong celebrations, young Singaporeans are treated to a huge street party complete with disk jockeys, dance music, and even disco lights and special effects.

Other annual events include Teacher's Day, when teachers receive recognition for their efforts during the year. On Children's Day and Youth Day, various outings, exhibitions, and concerts are held in honor of students. The more familiar Western commercial holidays of Valentine's Day, Mother's and Father's days, and New Year's Eve are also celebrated.

The *hongbao,* a packet containing money, is distributed during Chinese New Year.

Chocolate Easter eggs are very popular as in the West.

CALENDAR OF EVENTS

• JANUARY
NEW YEAR'S DAY The first day of the Christian year

• JANUARY / FEBRUARY
CHINESE NEW YEAR Most important Chinese festival, also referred to as the Lunar New Year or Spring Festival
CHINGAY PARADE Annual procession down the main shopping area marking the close of Chinese New Year celebrations
THAIPUSAM Hindu ritual of penance with *kavadi* processions between two temples

•FEBRUARY
VALENTINE'S DAY A day for lovers as in the West

• MARCH / APRIL
GOOD FRIDAY Remembering the crucifixion of Christ
EASTER Christian celebration of Christ's resurrection with processions and church services
FESTIVAL OF QING MING Chinese festival meaning "Clear and Bright" when dead family ancestors are honored by visits to the grave
HARI RAYA PUASA Sighting of the new moon and the end of the fasting month of *Ramadan* for Muslims

• MAY
LABOR DAY Day of rest for all workers
MOTHER'S DAY Western celebration for mothers

• MAY / JUNE
VESAK DAY Celebration of three stages in the life of Buddha, his birth, enlightenment, and death

• JUNE / JULY

DRAGON BOAT FESTIVAL Annual international race in decorated boats held in honor of the ancient poet, Qu Yan

HARI RAYA HAJI Muslim festival commemorating the annual pilgrimage of Muslims to the holy city of Mecca

YOUTH DAY Concerts, exhibitions, and parade held in honor of the youth of Singapore

FATHER'S DAY Western celebration of the father's role in society

• AUGUST

MARKET FESTIVAL Precursor to the Festival of the Hungry Ghosts when market stall-holders put on lavish feasts to ensure business will prosper in the coming year

FESTIVAL OF THE HUNGRY GHOSTS Chinese worship of souls released from purgatory

NATIONAL DAY Celebration of Singapore's independence

• SEPTEMBER

LANTERN/MOONCAKE/MID-AUTUMN FESTIVAL Chinese celebration of the moon

NAVRAATRI Hindu celebration in honor of the three consorts of the Hindu Trinity

• OCTOBER / NOVEMBER

CHILDREN'S DAY For all those under 12 years of age

THIMITHI Fire-walking festival of Hindus to fulfill vows

DEEPAVALI Hindu festival celebrating the victory of good over evil

MAULIDIN NABI Birthday of the Prophet Mohammed

• DECEMBER

CHRISTMAS Christian celebration of the birth of Christ

The *zong* ("djong"), a rice cake stuffed with meat, chestnuts, and egg yolks, symbolizes the rice mounds thrown into the river to save Qu Yan.

The *ketupat,* rice cake wrapped in coconut leaves, is traditionally served tor Hari Raya.

Indian lamp for Deepavali, the Hindu Festival of Lights.

FOOD

SINGAPORE IS UNIQUE in Southeast Asia for its great variety of cuisines, the most interesting of which have evolved from the traditions of early immigrants through settlement and intermarriage. While each culture kept up its traditional cooking, it could not help but absorb and modify food ideas from other immigrants with whom it came into contact. To define a typical Singapore cuisine would therefore be very difficult.

MAIN ETHNIC GROUPS AND THEIR CUISINES

THE CHINESE Although most Chinese migrants came to Singapore from southern China, they were a mixed people from a variety of provinces, each with its own distinctive cuisine. Their various cuisines were all simple meals centered on rice, though some wheat-based dishes, such as steamed dumplings and noodles, came from northern China. The resulting assortment of dishes grew in variety as they borrowed ideas from one another.

Pork is a favorite with the Chinese, followed by poultry and fish. Lamb is considered too "heavy," while beef in large quantities is thought to be bad for the body and is seldom eaten. Fresh vegetables play an important role. Indeed, all the ingredients must be fresh with only a little added seasoning, and amounts are balanced to provide both variety and texture.

Opposite: **The cuisine of Singapore's Malays is a blending of styles from all over the Malay world. Malay meals are based on rice with an assortment of spiced dishes including poultry, meat, and vegetables plus a condiment. Pork is never eaten, since Malays are Muslims.**

Below: **The fare of a typical Chinese hawker selling rice and various meat, seafood, and vegetable dishes**

Food in Singapore is said to be influenced by many sources. The famous *satay* (pieces of marinated chicken, beef, or mutton skewered and grilled) is a variation of the Middle Eastern *kebab*.

THE MALAYS When Islam came to the Malays in the 14th century, it was brought not by Arabs but by Indian Muslims from Gujarat in northwest India. From them, the Malays also inherited many Middle Eastern dishes with Indian influence.

Fish and chicken are eaten most often. Beef is enjoyed sometimes, mutton less often, and pork is forbidden to Muslims. Rice is the basis of a Malay meal, which will usually include vegetables with some fish, meat, or eggs and *sambal* ("sahm-bahl") accompaniments like a chutney or sauce.

THE PERANAKANS This is perhaps the only cuisine that can be said to be truly Singaporean, springing from a unique blend of Malay and Chinese cultures and developed by the Straits Chinese. However, it is time-consuming to prepare and, because of this, quickly disappearing in modern Singapore.

Chinese ingredients are used but taste quite different when Malay ingredients are added. Interestingly, the Straits Chinese adopted Malay customs and rituals but not their religion, so pork is eaten. Their pork *satay* is similar to the Malay dish but sweeter. Conversely, their cakes are much enjoyed by Singaporean Chinese whose food traditions do not place much emphasis on cakes or desserts.

An Indian Muslim food stall serving lunch

THE INDIANS The Tamils from the southeast Indian state of Tamil Nadu have always been a close-knit community, but food styles brought to Singapore by Indian traders from Madras, Kerala, Sri Lanka, Pakistan, Punjab, and Persia have had long-term effects on their cuisine.

Though strictly speaking Hindus are meant to be vegetarian and originally would not consume meat, fish, or even eggs, many now eat mutton and chicken, though not on Friday, which is a day of prayer. Some Hindus will not touch pork, not for religious reasons as much as because it is considered "unclean."

RECIPE FOR CURRY PUFFS

Singaporeans love snacks and the curry puff is one snack enjoyed by people from all walks of life. This recipe should make six.

Ingredients

100g (about 3^1/$_2$ ounces) pie crust pastry
beaten egg for glazing

Filling

1 tablespoon oil
half a large onion, chopped
1 dessert spoon of curry paste
1 small potato, boiled and diced
75g (about 2^1/$_2$ ounces) ground meat
^{1}/$_4$ teaspoon salt

Method

Heat the oil and saute the onion until light brown.
Add the curry paste and saute until fragrant.
Add the potato, ground meat, and salt.
Fry until the meat has been cooked, then put on a plate and let cool.
Roll out the dough thinly and cut out large circles.
Put a teaspoonful of the filling on each circle.
Wet the pastry edge with water and fold the pastry in half, sealing the edges.
Pinch the edges or press with a fork. Glaze with beaten egg.
Bake at 210° C (400°F) on the top shelf for 20 minutes or until golden brown.

THE EURASIANS In Singapore, Eurasians are generally people of Portuguese and Indian or Sri Lankan descent whose food is a combination of East and West. Many dishes have their origins in Goa, which was a Portuguese area of India. Wine and sherry are added to their curries and seasonings make their olive oil hot and spicy. Their cuisine, like the Peranakan, is slowly dying away as more Eurasians marry the other Asian ethnic groups of Singapore.

FAVORITE SINGAPOREAN FOOD

CHINESE
CHICKEN RICE Small pieces of sliced chicken served with rice cooked in chicken stock and flavored with chilies, ginger, and soy sauce.
FRIED *KWAY TEOW* Large flat rice noodles, fried with a mixture of prawns, pork, cockles, and bean sprouts.
DIM SUM Lunchtime assortment of bite-sized dumplings, rolls, and buns, stuffed with a variety of meat, prawns, and vegetables, served hot in bamboo trays.

MALAY
SATAY Small pieces of meat on skewers, grilled over a charcoal fire; served with a peanut sauce, small packets of rice wrapped in coconut leaves, and sliced cucumbers and onions.
NASI PADANG Selection of meat, fish, and vegetable dishes, originally from Padang in West Sumatra. All are hot and spicy and served with plain rice.

PERANAKAN
CHILI CRAB Pieces of crab still in their shell, fried in a chili and soy sauce paste.
POPIAH Thin wheat flour pancake filled with shredded turnip, egg, prawns, garlic, and sprouts, served with sweet black sauce and hot sauce.
OTAK-OTAK Bundles of fish mixed with pounded spices and coconut milk, wrapped in coconut leaves and grilled over a charcoal fire.

INDIAN
THOSAI Paper-thin, slightly sour, rice flour and lentil pancake.
MURTABAK Savory pancake filled with lightly seasoned mutton or chicken and onion, served with a curry sauce and cucumbers topped with ketchup
FISH HEAD CURRY Large fish head cooked in a curry sauce.

FOODS AND THEIR SOURCES

Rice is an essential part of local meals, but, as none is grown in Singapore, it is imported from abroad. Noodles are also a favorite, especially as a snack. These are available freshly made or as an instant packaged variety.

Meat, fish, poultry, and bean curd are the main sources of protein. About 60% of the chickens and 90% of the ducks eaten are reared on special farms in the northwest part of the island; the rest are imported. The rearing of pigs has been phased out due to limited land space. Beef and mutton are brought in from Australia, New Zealand, and elsewhere.

Fish is caught and brought to the auction markets in the early hours of the morning. Since Singaporeans eat a lot of fish and other seafood, much of it still has to be imported.

Most Singaporeans shop in a "wet" market where fresh produce ranging from chickens to vegetables can be bought.

VARIETIES OF LOCAL FRUIT

DURIAN

This "king of fruits" is large and round with a tough skin covered with thick spikes. Inside, large seeds are enclosed in creamy flesh. Even its notorious smell, suggesting a gas leak, is considered delightful by local durian lovers.

MANGOSTEEN

A thick, hard, purplish black skin encloses tiny segments of sweet, white flesh.

RAMBUTAN

This is a small white-fleshed fruit enclosed in a bright red hairy skin. *(Rambut* means "hair" in Malay.)

PAPAYA

A bright orange oval-shaped fruit containing small black seeds, which are not eaten.

Most vegetable farms are in the northwest where there is less urban development, but, as Singapore's soil is not very fertile, hydroponic experiments are in progress to grow plants in nutrient-rich water without using soil. Nevertheless, 75% of all Singapore's vegetables come from Malaysia and other neighboring countries. Mainly green and leafy vegetables as well as tubers, water chestnuts, bamboo shoots, and bean sprouts are eaten.

Imported fresh fruit such as apples, oranges, pears, and grapes, as well as a great variety of tropical fruit, is available all year round in Singapore. Mangosteen, papaya, rambutan, and jackfruit are grown here, while mangoes, pineapples, and watermelons come from elsewhere in the region.

A great variety of tinned, packaged, and preserved foods are prepared in factories in Singapore as well as imported from abroad. Ingredients for many different cuisines are flown in daily.

Hydroponic farming methods use less land space.

THE KITCHEN GOD

The Kitchen God, Zao Chun ("djow choon"), is one of the Chinese household gods. He is represented by a piece of red paper inscribed with his name and hung in the kitchen, the center of family life.

The Kitchen God ascends to heaven each New Year and reports on the family hardships to the Jade Emperor. When he is sent off, one week before the Lunar New Year, Chinese believers offer him honey to sweeten his lips so that he will have only good things to say, or glutinous rice cakes to stick his lips together and prevent him from saying anything at all.

While he is away, the paper bearing his name is taken down and burned and a new one put up awaiting his return. Honor is paid to him by lighting incense sticks on an altar beneath his name.

An altar to the Kitchen God

KITCHENS

Kitchens tend to be very simply organized, and even fine meals are generally cooked with inexpensive, traditional utensils that continue to be favorites, along with the modern rice cooker and the microwave oven.

In a Singapore kitchen, a *kuali* ("kwah-lee") or wok is considered indispensable. This is a wide, bowl-like pan with a curving base and high, sloping sides. It is usually made of heavy iron. Stir- and deep-frying, steaming, and boiling are the preferred ways of cooking.

In addition to the wok, a *batu lesong* ("bah-too leh-sowng") is used. This is a hollowed-out granite bowl with a granite pestle for grinding seasonings such as onions, chilies, fresh turmeric, and garlic. Terracotta or clay pots are used in cooking because these are said to improve the taste of curries and are decorative as well as useful.

EATING HABITS

Rice is the basis of all meals and is accompanied by three to five other dishes and condiments. A Chinese meal will include soup, fish, something made with pork, and some vegetables. Each place setting will have a pair of chopsticks, a rice bowl, a small plate for the main course, and a tiny dish for sauces. In addition, there will be a teacup or glass for hot Chinese tea or iced water.

Malay families serve a fish or meat dish, a vegetable dish, and a chili *sambal,* usually in common serving dishes. In today's urban environment people will sit at a Western table, using forks and spoons, but many still use their hands to eat. Knives, which are considered to be weapons, are unnecessary since the food is always in bite-sized pieces.

Indian dishes follow a similar pattern to Malay ones, except for vegetarian meals that include a range of vegetable and lentil dishes. These are served with plain rice, pepper-water to wash it down, and a small serving of cool yogurt. Indian meals are sometimes served on square-cut banana leaves. A glass of cold water will be placed on the left since the right hand is used for eating.

A group of office workers having lunch at a hawker center

EATING OUT

It is possible to eat around the world in Singapore. It is hard to believe such a tiny island can offer Indian, Chinese, Arab, Japanese, Thai, Korean, and Vietnamese food, as well as almost all types of Western food, from top European restaurants in major hotels to American fast-food outlets in shopping centers.

Eating out at hotels and restaurants is comparatively expensive, but local food in hawker centers is inexpensive and very popular. Singaporeans can happily lunch in a foreign restaurant, snack at a hawker center, and then return to their own ethnic group's home cooking.

Hawker food differs from home-cooked and restaurant food in its

Right: **A round table dining at a Chinese restaurant. The food is placed in the middle and the diners take what they want.**

Opposite above: **Air-conditioned food courts are upmarket hawker centers and can normally be found in shopping centers in the city.**

Opposite below: **Each housing estate has its own hawker center. Because of their busy lifestyles, many Singaporeans prefer to eat out. These centers are open from early in the morning until past midnight for late-night eaters and shift-workers.**

114

simplicity and speed of preparation. Traveling hawkers once found this an easy way to earn a living. One-man mobile kitchens sold noodles, spring rolls, Indian breads with curry, fish porridge, and fruit juices. With the shift to a more urban lifestyle, they have been moved to permanent sites, but continue to be known as "hawkers."

Hawker complexes are little more than vast, noisy, open-air kitchens, but they have atmosphere and are less expensive than hotel coffeeshops. Each hawker stall has a large advertising signboard and may specialize in one type of food. All are licensed, and inspectors make regular checks to ensure high standards of health and cleanliness.

FOOD TABOOS

Muslims can only eat food that is *halal*("hahl-lal"), that is, conforms to their religious restrictions. Eating pork is forbidden as is the drinking of alcohol and eating meat that has not been slaughtered by another Muslim. Neither Muslims nor Indians eat with the left hand, although they do pass food around with this hand and use it to hold a glass.

Hindus are forbidden to eat beef because the cow is considered a sacred animal. Many Hindus are completely vegetarian because they believe they will experience a similar pain if they take the life of a living thing unnecessarily. These strict Hindus and Buddhists do not eat eggs either, because they are an animal product.

FOOD BELIEFS

The Chinese and Indians believe the type of food eaten creates a certain kind of person and that eating should be for both body and spirit. They also believe that gods eat too, and they offer food to the deities as a sign of respect, thanksgiving, and a way to ensure future blessings. Eating the food offered is a symbol of their communication with the god.

Most Singaporeans believe that food is "heaty" or "cooling," depending on its effect on the body. Examples of heaty foods are chocolate and meat. These make the body feel too hot, full, and uncomfortable. To counteract the upset they cause, cooling foods such as tomatoes, cucumber, water melon, or herbal soups are prescribed to restore "inner" balance. Illness can be caused by eating heaty foods, but cooling foods can also cause or aggravate colds and should not be eaten on cool days.

Opposite: **During the Festival of the Hungry Ghosts, long tables piled with food are set in temple grounds so that ghosts are not drawn to people's homes. Arranged around the tables are banners, candles, and images of gods. Bunches of joss sticks burn in large pots full of sand to protect the living and draw the gods nearer. Once the spirits have enjoyed the offerings and prayers have been said, the food is eaten by the community.**

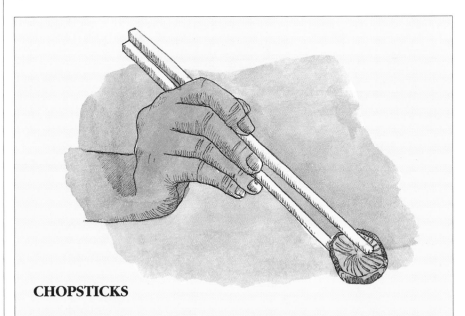

CHOPSTICKS

The first chopsticks of ancient China were probably twigs or bamboo sticks used to prevent fingers from getting burned. Since then, chopsticks have been made in wood, bone, ivory, jade, and silver. The emperors of China believed that if their food was poisoned, their silver chopsticks would become discolored.

Today, many Chinese families in Singapore use forks and spoons and only use chopsticks for certain dishes. Children begin using chopsticks at around 4 years of age for any food that is easy to pick up. They soon learn that food can also be pressed, pulled, and broken with them.

There is a chopstick etiquette to be learned too. It is rude to wave chopsticks while eating or to leave them stuck in a bowl of rice. They should not rest on the rice bowl; this is a sign that the food was not enough.

In Singapore, it is not unusual to see non-Chinese using chopsticks with ease.

TABLE MANNERS

The normal practice when serving food in homes is to place all the dishes in the center of the table at the beginning of the meal, so that people can help themselves as the meal progresses. It is important to take only what is needed because it is considered impolite to waste food.

In Chinese restaurants, one course is presented at a time. The Chinese like to eat as a communal group with an even number of diners, whereas in more conservative Malay and Indian homes, the men eat first, followed by the women.

Both Malays and Indians eat with the fingers of the right hand. The Malays scoop up a little food in the hollow of their bent fingers, never soiling the palm of their hand. Unlike the Malays, the Indians press and roll their food into a small ball using their fingers and palms and then carry it to the mouth with the fingertips. Sucking or licking the fingers is considered bad manners.

Hindus eating in a temple after prayers. Only the right hand is used and It is considered most impolite to use the left.

FEASTS

Chinese feasts can stretch to 12 courses: the more festive the occasion, the more courses that are offered. It is not polite to arrive on time since this will show greed. Guests usually leave immediately after the meal is finished to show they are satisfied. For the Chinese, all festivities take place during the meal, not after.

There is an art in selecting courses. They are chosen to harmonize with each other in taste, color, and texture. The first course is usually a cold appetizer, followed by some dry dishes, and then some with sauce. Spicy dishes are set against more subtle ones and the soft against the crispy. Filling soups, fried rice, or noodles are traditionally served during the second-to-last course, to ensure no guest goes home hungry.

A Malay feast is generally a dinner party held at home, a thanksgiving *kenduri,* or a wedding. Guests arrive on time or earlier and will even help with the preparations. *Nasi minyak* ("nah-see-mee-yah")—rice prepared with ghee, milk or yogurt, onions, and garlic—is commonly served at Malay weddings to symbolize prosperity. By tradition, guests at Malay weddings also receive wrapped and decorated eggs, symbols of fertility.

Muslims keep treats for the end of the fasting month, such as tarts filled with fresh pineapple jam or peanut biscuits. A range of foreign-influenced dishes are always served—*rendang daging* ("rehn-dahng dah-gehng"), a Sumatran dish of beef in coconut milk; *ayam korma* ("ah-yahm core-mah"), a chicken dish of Middle-Eastern origin; and Javanese *tempe* ("tam-pay"), fermented soybean cake, fried with fresh prawns and peanuts.

At Hindu wedding celebrations, people usually arrive on time and leave about half-an-hour after the feast. Vegetarian food will probably be served, set out on long tables. Sour rice must never be served at Hindu weddings and the dishes must not be too hot, too spicy, or salty because this foretells

Opposite: **Chinese cuisines share a number of common elements. The balancing of colors, textures, and flavors is of paramount importance.**

bad luck for the newlyweds.

North Indians are strictly vegetarian on Deepavali, whereas South Indians have a variety of meat dishes. Favorite festival foods are *muruku* ("moo-roo-koo"), a savory crisp of rice flour and spices; ghee balls, a mixture of ghee, ground green beans, brown sugar, and cashew nuts; and *kesari* ("kay-sah-ree"), made of semolina, ghee, cashew nuts, and raisins.

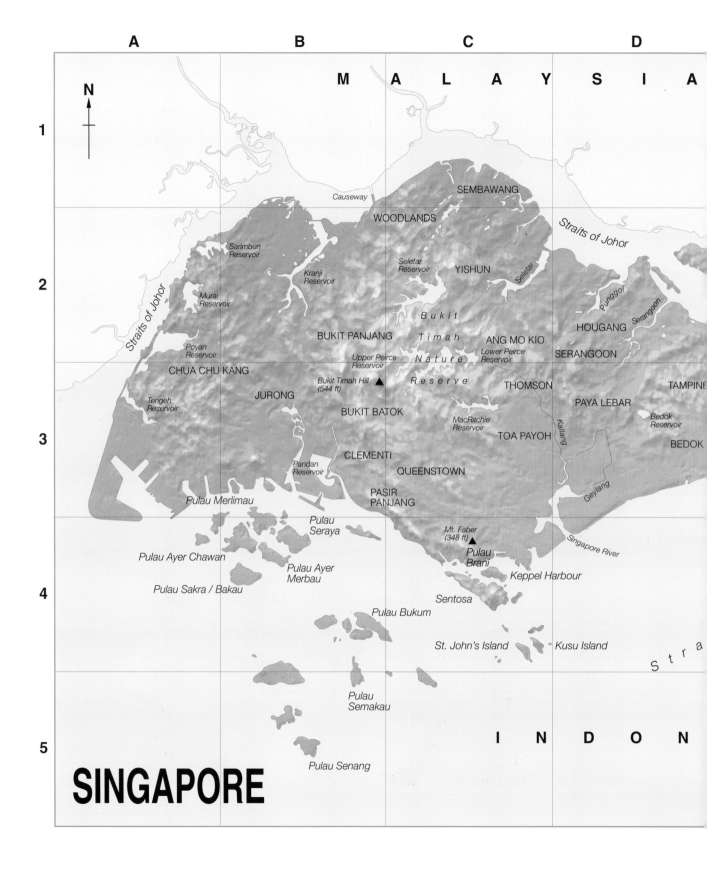

A   **B**   **C**   **D**

N

M A L A Y S I A

1

Causeway

*Sarimbun
Reservoir*

SEMBAWANG

WOODLANDS

Straits of Johor

*Seletar
Reservoir*

YISHUN

Seletar

*Kranji
Reservoir*

2

Straits of Johor

*Murai
Reservoir*

*Poyan
Reservoir*

BUKIT PANJANG

Bukit

Timah

ANG MO KIO

*Lower Peirce
Reservoir*

Punggol

Serangoon

HOUGANG

SERANGOON

*Upper Peirce
Reservoir*

Nature

CHUA CHU KANG

*Bukit Timah Hill
(544 ft)* ▲

Reserve

THOMSON

TAMPINE

*Tengeh
Reservoir*

JURONG

BUKIT BATOK

*MacRitchie
Reservoir*

PAYA LEBAR

*Bedok
Reservoir*

3

Kallang

TOA PAYOH

BEDOK

*Pandan
Reservoir*

CLEMENTI

QUEENSTOWN

Geylang

Pulau Merlimau

PASIR
PANJANG

*Pulau
Seraya*

*Mt. Faber
(348 ft)* ▲

*Pulau
Brani*

Singapore River

Pulau Ayer Chawan

*Pulau Ayer
Merbau*

Keppel Harbour

4

Pulau Sakra / Bakau

Sentosa

Pulau Bukum

St. John's Island

Kusu Island

S t r a

*Pulau
Semakau*

5

I N D O N

Pulau Senang

SINGAPORE

E   F

ulau Ubin

Pulau Tekong Reservoir

Pulau Tekong

CHANGI

of Singapore

S   I   A

Capital city
Major town
Mountain peak

Height of land (feet)
over 420
300 – 420
180 – 300
120 – 180
60 – 120
0 – 60

QUICK NOTES

AREA
247 square miles

POPULATION
2.87 million

NATIONAL FLOWER
Vanda Miss Joaquim, an orchid hybrid

NATIONAL SYMBOL
A legendary lion, red against a white background. The lion's mane has five partings representing democracy, peace, progress, justice, and equality.

NATIONAL ANTHEM
Majulah Singapura ("Let Singapore Flourish")

MAJOR RIVER
Seletar River

HIGHEST POINT
Bukit Timah Hill (544 feet)

CLIMATE
Hot and humid, with rainfall all year round. Average daily temperature 80°F

OFFICIAL LANGUAGES
Malay, Mandarin, Tamil, and English

MAJOR RELIGIONS
Taoism, Buddhism, Islam, Hinduism, Christianity

CURRENCY
100 cents make one Singapore dollar ($1 = S$1.6)

MAIN EXPORTS
Petroleum products, electronic products and components, chemicals, garments, personal computers, disk drives, printed circuits, and telecommunications apparatus

IMPORTANT ANNIVERSARY
National Day (August 9)

LEADERS IN POLITICS
Sir Thomas Stamford Raffles—founder of modern Singapore
Yusof bin Ishak—First Asian head of state (1959-1965), president of Singapore (1965-1970)
David Marshall—First chief minister (1955-1956)
Benjamin Sheares—President of Singapore (1971-1981)
Lee Kuan Yew—Prime minister (1959-1990)
Goh Chok Tong—Prime minister since 1990
Ong Teng Cheong—President since 1993

GLOSSARY

animism   Belief that all natural objects (rocks, trees, etc.) possess souls.

Confucianism   System of ethics named after the Chinese philosopher, Confucius, that formed the basis of society, education, and administration in China.

durian   Large, round fruit with a tough skin covered in thick spikes. Inside, large seeds are enclosed in creamy flesh. Despite its smell, which has been compared to a gas leask, it is affectionately known as the "king of fruits."

geomancy   Chinese natural science of living in harmony with nature to ensure a good life.

halal   ("hahl-lal") The word used to describe food prepared in accordance with the laws of Islam, the religion of the Muslims.

Hanyu Pinyin   ("han-yoo pin-yin") A standardized way of writing the Chinese language in the Roman script used by English.

hawker   One who sells food from a stall; a hawker center is a place where many hawkers are located.

Hindu trinity   This refers to the three most important gods—Brahma (the Creator), Vishnu (the Preserver), and Shiva (the Destroyer).

hongbao   ("hong-pao") Small gift packets containing money, especially used at Chinese New Year.

joss stick   Slender stick of fragrant paste burned by Chinese, Indians, and others, as incense for religious rituals.

Peranakan   ("Per-ran-nah-kan") Chinese born in the region who spoke Baba Malay, a mixture of Malay and the Hokkien dialect of Chinese.

sambal   ("sahm-bahl") Spicy accompaniment made from ground chilies served with rice.

Singlish   A form of English unique to Singapore that uses Chinese and Malay words and grammatical patterns.

songkok   ("song-kok") A traditional hat worn by Malay boys and men, usually on special occasions.

sultan   Malay royal ruler.

BIBLIOGRAPHY

Hoe, Irene. *Singapore*. Passport Books, Illinois, 1989.

Insight Guide. *Singapore*. Houghton Mifflin, Boston, 1994.

Lloyd, Ian and Schafer, Betty. *Singapore*. Times Editions, Singapore 1989.

Wee, Jessie. *Let's Visit Singapore*. Burke, Connecticut, 1985.

INDEX

INDEX

INDEX

Picture Credits

Mazlan Badron, Sheila Brown, Wendy Chan, Andrew Chin, Jonathan Choo, Barbara Dare, Jane Duff, Tackie Ho, Hui Man Yan, Aziz Hussin, Jimmy Kang, Simon Ker, Kenneth Koh, Peter Korn, Steven Lee, Michael Liew, Lim Kheng Chye, Philip Lim, Lim Seng Tiong, Chris Loh, Majlis Ugama Islam Singapura, National Archives, Raymond Ng, Nghai Chee Wah, Photobank, K.F. Seetoh, Singapore Tourist Promotion Board, David Tan, Tan Suan Ann, The New Paper, The Straits Times, and various Singapore government statutory boards and ministries.